Building Bridges

Content and Learning Strategies for ESL

**Anna Uhl Chamot
J. Michael O'Malley
Lisa Küpper**

Heinle & Heinle Publishers
A Division of Wadsworth, Inc.
Boston, MA 02116

HH

Publisher: Stanley J. Galek
Editorial Director: Christopher Foley
Project Coordinator: Anita L. Raducanu
Assistant Editor: Erik Gundersen
Copy Editor: Kathleen Sands Boehmer
Production Supervisor: Patricia Jalbert
Manufacturing Coordinator: Lisa McLaughlin
Internal Design: Caryl Hull Design Group
Cover Design: The Graphics Studio/Gerry Rosentswieg
Illustrator: Marcy Dunn Ramsey
Maps: FinalCopy Electronic Publishing Services
Photos: All photos by Jeff Greenberg, except: pp. 13, 15 Courtesy of NASA;
p. 23 Courtesy of Greater Miami Convention & Visitors Bureau; p. 71 Robert Perron

Acknowledgments

The authors and publisher would like to acknowledge the contributions of the following individuals who reviewed the *Building Bridges* program at various stages of development and who offered many helpful insights and suggestions:

CONSULTANTS

- Lydia Stack
  San Francisco Unified School District

- Michele R. Hewlett-Gomez
  Texas Education Agency

- Jacqueline Moase-Burke
  Oakland (MI) Intermediate School District

- Richard Hurst
  Holbrook (AZ) Public Schools

REVIEWERS

- Stephen F. Sloan
  Los Angeles Unified School District

- Carol A. Seagren
  Los Angeles Unified School District

- Toni Sachs Hadi
  New York City Public Schools

- Carol Anastasi
  Boston Public Schools

- Jennifer Bixby
  ESL Specialist

- Charlotte B. Seeley
  Newton (MA) Public Schools

Grateful acknowledgment is also made to Linda M. Cohen, Donna Gleason O'Neill, Jeffrey H. Schwartz, and Linda P. Smith for their early research and writing contributions to this project.

ISBN: 0-8384-1845-7

10 9 8 7 6

CONTENTS

UNIT	PAGE	CONTENT KNOWLEDGE	LEARNING STRATEGIES	LANGUAGE SKILLS
6 Regions of the World	71	Geographical regions of the world: climate, natural vegetation, animals	Use what you know ▪ Make inferences ▪ Take notes using Ideas Maps and T-lists ▪ Listen selectively	Present tense to describe and to talk about facts ▪ *Adjective* + *noun* to describe
7 Living Things	82	Cells and growth ▪ Characteristics of living things ▪ Some differences between plants and animals	Use what you know ▪ Take notes using an Idea Map and a diagram ▪ Listen selectively ▪ Cooperate	Present tense to describe and to talk about facts ▪ Past tense to talk about past events
8 Living in the United States	95	Personal rights and responsibilities ▪ Laws ▪ Democracy as a form of government ▪ Societal rights and responsibilities	Use what you know ▪ Make inferences ▪ Listen selectively ▪ Take notes ▪ Read selectively	*Should* + verb ▪ *Can* + verb ▪ *Have/has to* + verb ▪ Using *because* to give reasons
9 The Beginning of History	107	Timelines ▪ B.C. and A.D. ▪ First Americans ▪ Early civilizations ▪ Map skills	Use what you know ▪ Make a timeline ▪ Read selectively ▪ Make inferences ▪ Classify ▪ Cooperate	Past tense statements ▪ Simple present to state facts
10 Folktales of the World	121	Using literary analysis ▪ Interpreting a folktale	Use what you know ▪ Make inferences ▪ Take notes using a T-list ▪ Listen selectively ▪ Make predictions	*Be* + *going to* + verb to make predictions ▪ *Did* + subject + verb to ask questions about the past

PREFACE

TO THE TEACHER

Building Bridges: *Content and Learning Strategies for ESL* is a ground-breaking, three-level series designed to prepare secondary ESL students for success in academic subject areas. The series is based on the Cognitive Academic Language Learning Approach (CALLA), in which high-priority content, academic language development, and direct instruction in learning strategies are integrated into lessons that encourage student analysis and critical thinking.

Building Bridges may be used independently as a core series or in conjunction with Heinle & Heinle's **Intercom 2000,** whose focus on social/interactive language complements **Building Bridges'** focus on academic language and skills. **Building Bridges** can also be used to enhance other basic ESL series.

BUILDING BRIDGES Levels		Content
Book 1	High Beginning	• school survival • community life • academic language • learning strategies
Book 2	Low Intermediate	• major concepts and academic language associated with math, science, social studies, and literature • learning strategies
Book 3	Intermediate	

ANCILLARY COMPONENTS

Teacher's Manual

This easy-to-use resource for instructors provides general guidelines for teaching academic content, learning strategies, and language skills. In addition, detailed notes for each student text page give the instructor practical advice on how to present and practice new material.

Tests covering all material in the student texts appear at the end of each Teacher's Manual.

The Teacher's Manual further serves the practical needs of the teacher by providing answers to all *Practice* activities and scripts for all listening tasks.

Activity Masters

Diagrams, charts, maps, and other selected *Presentation* and *Practice* material are reproduced on duplicating masters. A special graphic symbol ( ) marks each chart, diagram, and map in the text that is reproduced. The Activity Masters also include additional practice materials.

Tape Program

Recordings of all mini-lectures on content topics may be heard on the tapes that accompany **Building Bridges.** A cassette symbol marks each section that is recorded.

ACADEMIC CONTENT IN BUILDING BRIDGES

Building Bridges is content-driven. That is to say, academic language skills are practiced as they occur in association with curriculum content, rather than in isolation.

The content topics in **Building Bridges** have been carefully selected from major topics and themes in the different subject areas. State curriculum frameworks, school district curricula, advice from content teachers, and widely-adopted secondary textbooks for each content area provided guidelines for content selection. All of the content topics provide students with opportunities to think and reflect on relationships between their own cultural background and American secondary school curricula.

Science topics are chosen from the biological sciences, health sciences, earth and space science, and physical science.

Mathematics units focus on developing problem-solving strategies with word problems. Students learn how to move beyond simple computation towards the development of reasoning skills that enable them to see different paths to successful problem solution.

Social studies topics include United States and world geography, civics, and an introduction to U.S. and world history.

In the literature units, students learn elements of literary analysis and reading strategies as they read and discuss fables, folktales, myths, and poetry from around the world.

LEARNING STRATEGIES IN *BUILDING BRIDGES*

The purpose of learning strategy instruction in **Building Bridges** is two-fold:

- to develop students' awareness of themselves as learners
- to provide students with techniques to assist them in mastering academic content and language.

When a learning strategy is introduced, an explanation of its rationale and applications is provided. Later, students are reminded when the strategy can be used with a similar activity. Teachers should introduce one strategy at a time by modeling the use of the strategy, describing its purpose, and discussing with students the names of the learning strategies and how to use them. (The Teacher's Manual provides guidance.) After completing an activity, students should discuss and reflect on the learning strategies they used.

Major learning strategies presented and practiced in **Building Bridges** are:

- using prior knowledge
- using selective attention in listening and reading
- taking notes
- making inferences from context
- grouping and classifying information
- using resources
- working cooperatively with classmates

LANGUAGE SKILLS IN *BUILDING BRIDGES*

Grammatical language skills are developed through *Language Skill* boxes that remind students of rules and usage relevant to the activities requiring specific grammatical structures.

UNIT STRUCTURE

- *Preparation:* Each unit begins with an activity designed to activate students' prior knowledge about the topic.
- *Presentation:* These sections teach new content information and learning strategies through reading and listening activities.
- *Practice:* In these activities, students actively use the new information they've learned in the *Presentation* sections. Students answer questions or solve problems, and then check the accuracy of their own work, often in cooperation with classmates. All four language skills are practiced, but the focus is on speaking and writing.
- *Extension:* Students integrate and apply the academic content and learning strategies that they have learned and practiced throughout the unit.
- *Learning Log:* Students evaluate their own success by completing the log that appears at the end of each unit.

Building Bridges provides students with a solid foundation in the content knowledge, academic language skills, and learning strategies they need to be successful in the all-English curriculum.

Because **Building Bridges** is based on the Cognitive Academic Language Learning Approach (CALLA), students are provided with experiences that engage their high-level thinking skills as they use the English language for authentic academic purposes.

Observation in Science

CONTENT KNOWLEDGE

Observation through the five senses ▪ The Scientific Method ▪ Conducting an experiment

LEARNING STRATEGIES

Use what you know ▪ Make inferences ▪ Read selectively ▪ Cooperate

LANGUAGE SKILLS

Present continuous ▪ Simple present ▪ Past tense statements and questions: regular and irregular verbs

Observing with your five senses

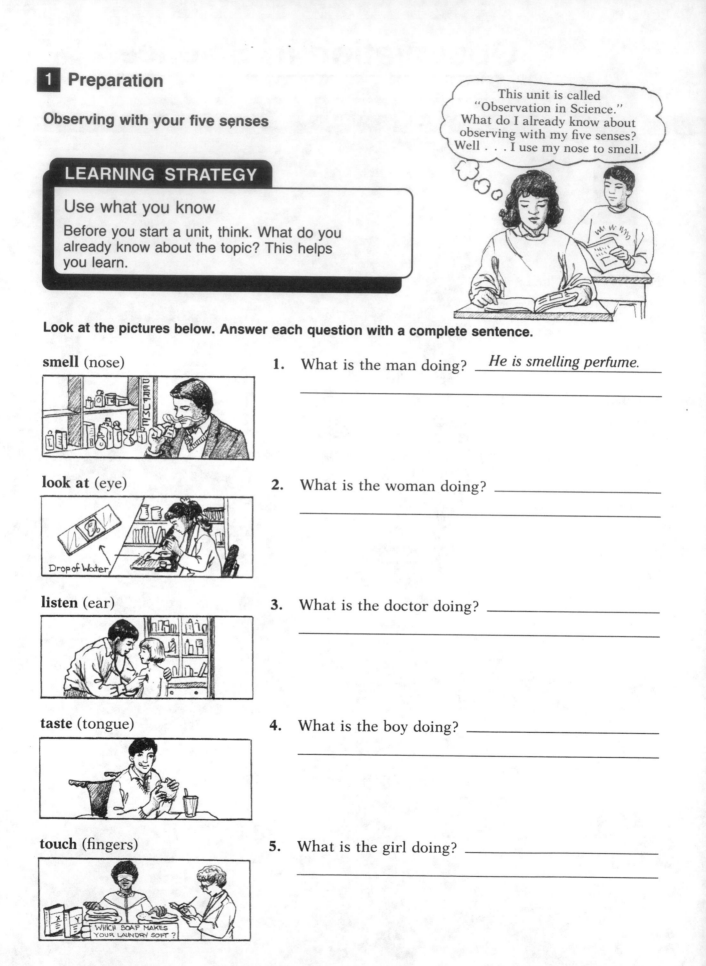

This unit is called "Observation in Science." What do I already know about observing with my five senses? Well . . . I use my nose to smell.

Look at the pictures below. Answer each question with a complete sentence.

smell (nose)

1. What is the man doing? _He is smelling perfume._ _____

look at (eye)

2. What is the woman doing? _____

listen (ear)

3. What is the doctor doing? _____

taste (tongue)

4. What is the boy doing? _____

touch (fingers)

5. What is the girl doing? _____

2 Presentation

Learn about the senses

The Five Senses

	BODY PART	VERBS	NAME OF SENSE
	eye(s)	see look at	sight
	nose	smell	smell
	ear(s)	hear listen	hearing
	tongue	taste	taste
	finger(s) hand(s)	touch feel	touch

3 Practice

Complete the sentences with words from the chart and its title.

When you use your eyes, your ears, your ___*nose*___ , your
fingers, and your tongue, you are using your (1) _____ .
You have five senses: smell, (2) _____ , hearing, taste, and
(3) _____ . You use your nose to (4) _____ . You
use your eyes to (5) _____ . For example, you use your
eyes to (6) _____ pictures in a book. You use your
(7) _____ to hear. For example, you use your ears to
(8) _____ to music. You use your (9) _____ to
taste. And to touch, you use your (10) _____ . You can also
use your (11) _____ to touch.

Look at the pictures of the teacher and students below. Write the name of the sense used to observe in each activity: *sight, smell, touch, hearing, taste.*

1. _____

2. _____

3. _____

4. _____

5. _____

6. _____

7. _____

8. _____

9. _____

5 **Presentation**

Read about observation in science

 We use **microscopes** to look at very small things.

We use **telescopes** to look at things that are very far away.

Observation

We learn about the world when we look, listen, smell, taste, and touch. We know many things about the world. But there are many things we don't know.

Scientists study the world. They want answers. They want to solve problems. They look, listen, smell, taste, and touch. In other words, they *observe* the world with their senses. They also make observations with instruments, such as microscopes and telescopes. They observe and they take notes on their observations. Observation is important in science. If we do not observe our world, we cannot learn about it and we cannot solve problems.

6 Practice AM

Answer the questions below with complete sentences. Use the simple present in 1, 3, 5, 6, and 7. Use the present continuous in 2 and 4.

> ┤ **LANGUAGE SKILLS** ├
>
> 1. Use the *simple present* to make general statements.
>
>   Scientists **study** the world.
>   The scientist **makes** an observation.
>
> 2. Use the *present continuous* to make statements about a situation that is happening now.
>
>   The scientist **is looking** in a microscope.
>   You **are learning** about science.

1. The scientist makes an observation. Then what does the scientist do?
   The scientist takes notes on his/her observation.

2. Look at the pictures on page 2 in this unit. Which people are taking notes on their observations? _____

3. Think. Why does a scientist take notes? Give two reasons.
   a. _____
   b. _____

4. Which people below are using **observation** to find out about the world? Write the letters. _____

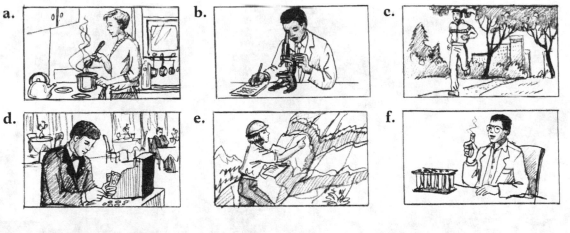

a.   b.   c.

d.   e.   f.

5. How do we observe the world? _____
   _____

6. Why do we observe the world? _____
   _____

7. What does a scientist do? _____
   _____

A. How do you use your five senses every day? Complete the chart by writing a sentence about how *you* use each sense.

> *I use the sense of sight when I watch television.*

SENSE	HOW I USE THIS SENSE
sight	
hearing	
smell	
touch	
taste	

B. Interview a classmate. Ask: How do you use your sense of _____ every day? Then write how your classmate uses the five senses.

SENSE	HOW MY CLASSMATE USES THIS SENSE
sight	
hearing	
smell	
touch	
taste	

8 Presentation

Find out about the Scientific Method

> **LEARNING STRATEGY**
>
> **Make inferences**
> Use word clues to guess meanings of new words. Word clues are the words before and after the new word.

> What does *disease* mean? Let's see . . . I'll look at the next sentence for a word clue . . . Oh, it must mean *sickness*.

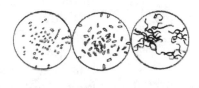

Malaria: A Serious Health Problem

Malaria is a serious disease. A person with malaria feels very cold at first, and then gets a high fever. If the person does not get medicine, this disease can be deadly. In the past, millions of people died from malaria. There was malaria in most parts of the world, including the United States.

Scientists knew some facts about malaria and about other diseases. These were the facts:

(1) Malaria occurs in low, wet areas of the world.
(2) Bacteria cause many diseases.

Scientists wanted to solve the problem of malaria. They used the Scientific Method to solve this problem.

> **WORD BOX**
>
> **Bacteria** are very small living things.
> You can see bacteria only with a microscope.
> (Bacteria is a plural form.)

9 Practice

Answer the questions with complete sentences.

1. Why is malaria a dangerous disease?
    Malaria is a dangerous disease because _____

2. How does a person with malaria feel?
    _____

3. How can people die from malaria?
    _____

4. In what areas of the world is there a lot of malaria?
    _____

5. What do bacteria look like? How can you see them?
    _____

Find out more about the Scientific Method

The Scientific Method Can Solve Problems

There are four steps in the Scientific Method.

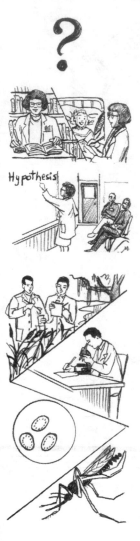

STEP 1: **Ask the question.**
What causes malaria?

STEP 2: **Make a *hypothesis*, or good guess.**
a.   Bacteria probably cause malaria.
b.   Malaria bacteria probably live in low, wet areas.
c.   Maybe bacteria are in the water. OR
d.   Maybe they live somewhere else.

STEP 3: **Make observations.**
Scientists tasted water from low, wet areas. They did not get malaria. Scientists used a microscope to examine the blood of malaria patients. They saw special bacteria in the blood of people with malaria. People without malaria did not have these special bacteria. Scientists observed some low, wet areas. They saw many mosquitos. They examined the mosquitos and found malaria bacteria. When the mosquitos with malaria bacteria bit people, the people got malaria.

STEP 4: **Answer the question.**
People get malaria from mosquitos with malaria bacteria.

This was how scientists solved the problem of malaria. They used the Scientific Method. Today we kill mosquitos in wet areas so that they cannot give malaria bacteria to people. Today many parts of the world are free from malaria.

11 Practice AM

Now answer these questions.

1. Put the steps of the Scientific Method in order.

   _____ Make observations.

   _____ Ask a question.

   _____ Answer the question.

   _____ Make a good guess, or *hypothesis*.

2. What was the question about malaria in *10 Presentation?*

   _____ Do people die from malaria?   _____ Is the hypothesis right?

   _____ What causes malaria?   _____ What is good medicine for malaria?

3. Scientists made observations (STEP 3) and took notes. List the observations.

   _____

   _____

4. Scientists used two of their senses. Which ones? _____

12 Presentation 🎞

LEARNING STRATEGY

Read selectively

Know what information you are reading for. Pay attention to key words. This helps you understand.

WORD BOX	
bright:	full of light. Red and yellow are **bright** colors.
dull:	not bright. Gray and black are **dull** colors.

Using the Scientific Method

Mr. Hernandez has a clothing store. He wants to sell lots of clothes. But he has to know—do people like bright colors such as red and yellow, or do they like dull colors, such as gray and black? He looks at the people in his store. He thinks, "They like bright colors. I see them wearing bright colors." But he's not sure.

So he talks to 100 customers. He asks them the same question: "Do you like clothes with bright colors or dull colors?" He writes down their answers. Then he looks at his notes. And guess what? Seventy-nine people like bright colors, and twenty-one like dull colors.

Work with a partner. Find the four steps of the Scientific Method in *12 Presentation*.

STEP 1: **Ask the question.**
Do people like
_____

STEP 2: **Make a hypothesis (a good guess).**
_____

STEP 3: **Make observations.**
_____

STEP 4: **Answer the question.**
_____

 **Extension** AM

Conduct a science experiment

Work with two or three other students to conduct an experiment.

LEARNING STRATEGY

Cooperate

When you *cooperate,* or work with other students, you can learn more.

Experiment With Lima Bean Seeds

1. **Ask the question:** What helps seeds grow?
2. **Make a hypothesis (a good guess):**
   The things that help a seed grow are: _____
   _____
   _____

3. **Make observations: Conduct an experiment**

   You need these things for your group's experiment:

   48 lima bean seeds 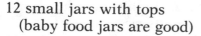   14 paper towels

   12 small jars with tops   lamp
      (baby food jars are good)

   glass bowl   refrigerator

   12 blank mailing labels   dark place

   DRAWER   CLOSET

Directions for the Experiment

a. Put the 48 lima bean seeds in the glass bowl. Fill with water. Leave the seeds in the water for 12 hours.

b. Prepare twelve labels. Mark the labels like this: Put the labels on the jars.

c. Fold a paper towel and put one in each jar. (Use 1/2 paper towel for small jars.)

d. Put some water on the paper towels in the jars with the WET label.

e. Dry the lima bean seeds in 2 paper towels.

f. Put 4 seeds in each jar (both WET and DRY jars). The seeds have to touch the folded paper towels.

g. Fix the 12 jars like this:

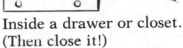

Under the lamp. (Light on!)   Inside the refrigerator. (Then close the door!)   Inside a drawer or closet. (Then close it!)

h. Wait for 2 days. Then examine the jars. Write what you see.

DRY jars under lamp _____

WET jars under lamp _____

DRY jars in refrigerator _____

WET jars in refrigerator _____

DRY jars in dark place _____

WET jars in dark place _____

i. Continue your observation. What do you see . . .

After 4 days? _____

After 1 week? _____

After 2 weeks? _____

After 3 weeks? _____

4. Answer the question: What helps seeds grow?

A. Work with your group. Write a short paragraph to answer the question.

_____

_____

_____

_____

B. Compare your group's answer to the answers of other groups.

UNIT 1: Learning Log

Check what you know. *Review* what you need to learn.

VOCABULARY

Five Senses

Nouns	Verbs
__ ear	__ feel
__ eye	__ hear
__ finger	__ listen
__ hand	__ look at
__ hearing	__ observe
__ nose	__ see
__ sight	__ smell
__ smell	__ taste
__ taste	__ touch
__ tongue	
__ touch	

Other Science Words

__ bacteria
__ blood
__ disease
__ experiment
__ fever
__ instruments
__ malaria
__ medicine
__ microscope
__ mosquito
__ observation
__ patient
__ telescope

Other Useful Verbs

__ cause
__ die
__ examine
__ kill
__ occur

The Scientific Method

__ 1. Ask the question.
__ 2. Make a hypothesis.
__ 3. Make observations.
__ 4. Answer the question.

Adjectives

__ bright	__ dull
__ dangerous	__ high
__ deadly	__ serious

LEARNING STRATEGIES

I can:

__ Use what I know about the senses to understand new information.
__ Make inferences to guess meanings of new words.
__ Read selectively by looking for key words.
__ Cooperate with classmates on a science experiment.

CONTENT AND LANGUAGE

I can:

__ Identify and talk about the five senses.
__ Use the present continuous to write about the five senses.
__ Read about observation in science and answer questions using the simple present.
__ Write about the senses I use for observation in my own life.
__ Read about the Scientific Method and the problem of malaria, and answer questions using the past tense.
__ Read about observation and the Scientific Method.
__ Conduct a science experiment using the Scientific Method.
__ Write about the procedures and results of a science experiment.

SELF-CHECK QUESTIONS

What is interesting in Unit 1?

_____

_____

What is easy?

_____

_____

What is difficult?

_____

_____

How can you learn what is difficult?

_____

_____

Mapping the Earth

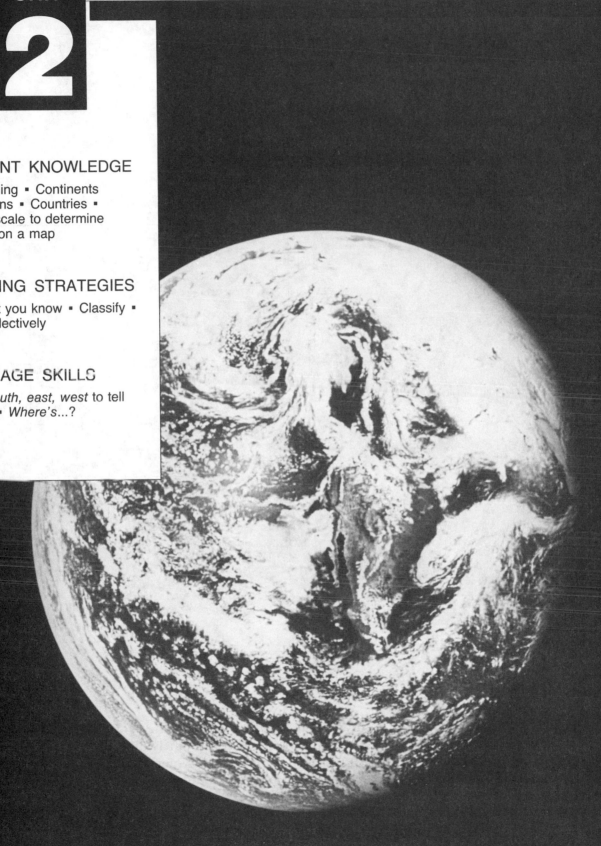

CONTENT KNOWLEDGE

Map reading • Continents and oceans • Countries • Using a scale to determine distance on a map

LEARNING STRATEGIES

Use what you know • Classify • Listen selectively

LANGUAGE SKILLS

North, south, east, west to tell location • *Where's...?*

Look at a world map

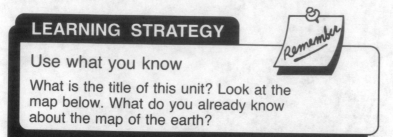

Map of the World

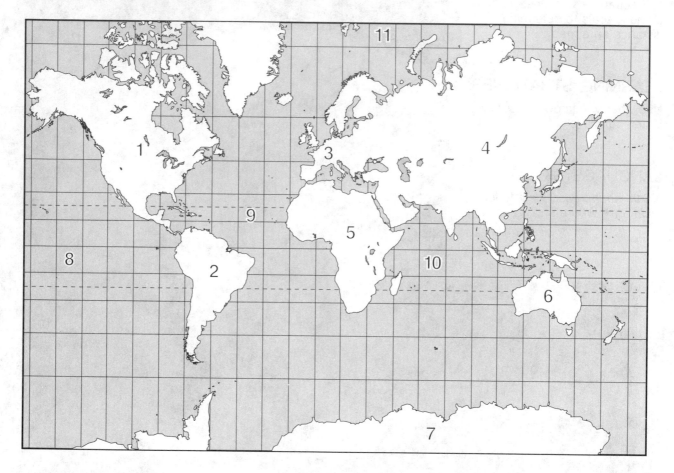

A.   Read about continents and oceans of the world.

The earth is made up of land and water. When we map the earth, we divide the land into seven **continents.** A continent is a large body of land, such as North America. (Find North America on the map. It is labelled **1.**) One continent usually has many different countries.

An **ocean** is a large body of water. Oceans cover three-fourths, or 75 percent, of the earth. The earth has four oceans. The biggest is the Pacific Ocean. (Find the Pacific Ocean on the map. It is labelled **8.**)

B. The continents and the oceans of the world are numbered on the map. Use the *World Word Box.* First write the names of the continents and oceans. Then find your country on the map.

WORLD WORD BOX			
Europe	South America	Pacific Ocean	Antarctica
Australia	Atlantic Ocean	Arctic Ocean	~~North America~~
Indian Ocean	Asia	Africa	

CONTINENTS OF THE EARTH

1. *North America*
2. _____
3. _____
4. _____
5. _____
6. _____
7. _____

OCEANS OF THE EARTH

8. _____
9. _____
10. _____
11. _____

Read a map

When we map the earth, we divide the continents into smaller pieces and give them names. Here is a map of North America, Central America, and South America. Study the map. Find the names of the countries you know.

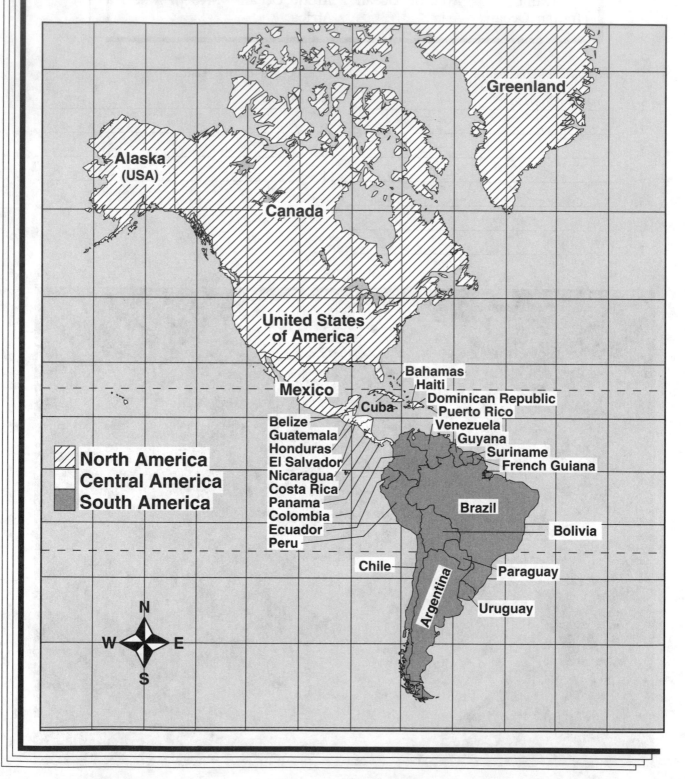

3 Practice AM

LEARNING STRATEGY

Classify

When you classify things, you put them into groups. *Classifying* is a good way to organize information. Put things that are alike into the same group.

Unclassified	Classified
□ ○ △ ▢ ○ ○ △ ○ △ ▢	Triangles △ △ △ Squares ▢ ▢ ▢ Circles ○ ○ ○

Classify the words in the Country Box into the groups *North America*, *Central America*, and *South America*. Use the map on page 16 to help you.

COUNTRY BOX

~~Peru~~	Mexico	United States of America	Uruguay
Canada	Brazil	Costa Rica	Suriname
Honduras	Colombia	Guatemala	Panama

NORTH AMERICA

_____

_____

_____

_____

CENTRAL AMERICA

_____

_____

_____

_____

SOUTH AMERICA

Peru

_____

_____

_____

4 Practice AM

Use the map on page 16 to complete the sentences.

LANGUAGE SKILL

Use **north/south/east/west of** to tell location.

Mexico is **south** of the United States.

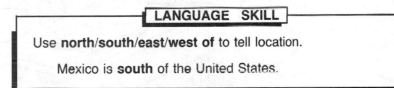

1. Peru is _____ of Ecuador.
2. Brazil is _____ of Peru.
3. Canada is _____ of the United States.
4. Guatemala is _____ of El Salvador.
5. Mexico is _____ of the West Indies.
6. Chile is west of _____ .
7. Guatemala is south of _____ .
8. Suriname is east of _____ .
9. Paraguay is north of _____ .
10. Colombia is west of _____ .

5 Practice

Use the map on page 16 to write your own sentences. Make sure you use the direction words *north*, *south*, *east*, and *west*.

1. _The United States is south of Canada._
2. _____
3. _____
4. _____
5. _____
6. _____

6 Practice

Listen to the tape. The speaker is talking about his country. Circle what the speaker tells you. Then look at the map on page 16. Where is his country?

LEARNING STRATEGY

Listen selectively

Before you listen, look at the words below. This helps you get ready to listen. Be ready to circle the words you hear.

I have to circle the words I hear. Let me look at the words now, so I'll be ready to hear them. OK, North America, South America . . .

1. My country is in . . .   North America / South America / Central America / Caribbean Islands

2. Neighboring countries . . .   Brazil / Colombia / Peru / Argentina / Venezuela / Panama / Puerto Rico

3. To the east is . . .   Peru / the Atlantic Ocean / the Caribbean / Venezuela / Argentina

4. Main export is . . .   bananas / coffee / emeralds / oil

5. Guess my country.   _____

Read a map

Here is a map of Europe, Asia, Africa, and Australia. Study the
map. Find the names of countries you know.

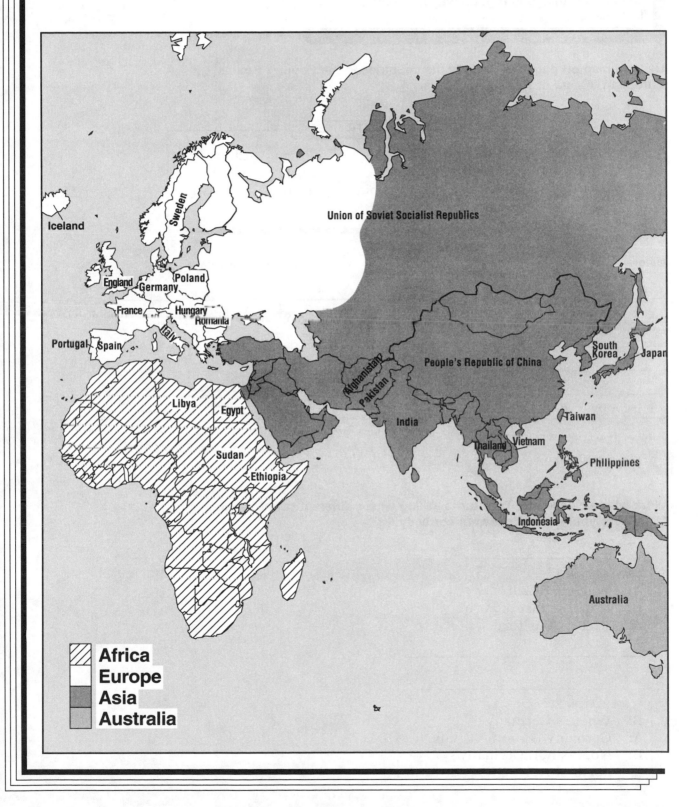

8 Practice AM

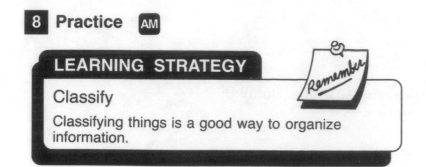
Use the map on page 19. Classify the countries in the Country Box as European, Asian, or African countries.

```
┌─────────────── COUNTRY BOX ───────────────┐
│                                            │
│   Italy        Libya      Vietnam   China  │
│   Philippines  India      Spain     Thailand │
│   Sweden       Ethiopia   Hungary   Germany │
│   Portugal     Egypt      Korea            │
│                                            │
└────────────────────────────────────────────┘
```

EUROPE	ASIA	AFRICA
Italy		

9 Practice

Work with a classmate. Take turns asking where different countries are. Make sure your partner answers correctly.

CONVERSATION 1
A: Where's Brazil?
B: Brazil is **east** of Peru.
A: Right. Your turn.

CONVERSATION 2
B: Where's Germany?
A: Germany is **south** of Italy.
B: No, it's not. Germany's **north** of Italy. OK, your turn.

---

10 Presentation and Practice 🔲

Learn more direction words

LEARNING STRATEGY

Use what you know

Remember to use what you know about direction words.

You know the words **north, south, east**, and **west.** But there are other words that tell location. When a place isn't exactly to the north, south, east, or west, we use words such as **northwest, southwest, northeast**, and **southeast. Northwest**, for example, is between **north** and **west.**

Label the arrows for the picture. Use the words *northwest, southwest, northeast,* **and** *southeast.*

ARROW 1: _____   ARROW 3: _____

ARROW 2: _____   ARROW 4: _____

11 Practice 🆎

Each item below lists three countries. Using the maps in this unit, go in a straight line from country 1 to country 2 to country 3. What direction are you going? Answer using the words *northwest, southwest, northeast,* **or** *southeast.*

1. England to Italy to Egypt   *southeast*
2. Japan to India to Ethiopia   _____
3. Libya to Iran to China   _____
4. India to Pakistan to Italy   _____
5. Mexico to Colombia to Brazil   _____
6. Brazil to Paraguay to Chile   _____
7. Bolivia to Colombia to U.S.   _____
8. Argentina to Brazil to Europe   _____
9. Canada to U.S. to Suriname   _____
10. Vietnam to Iran to Europe   _____

Read details on a map

Map of the U.S.

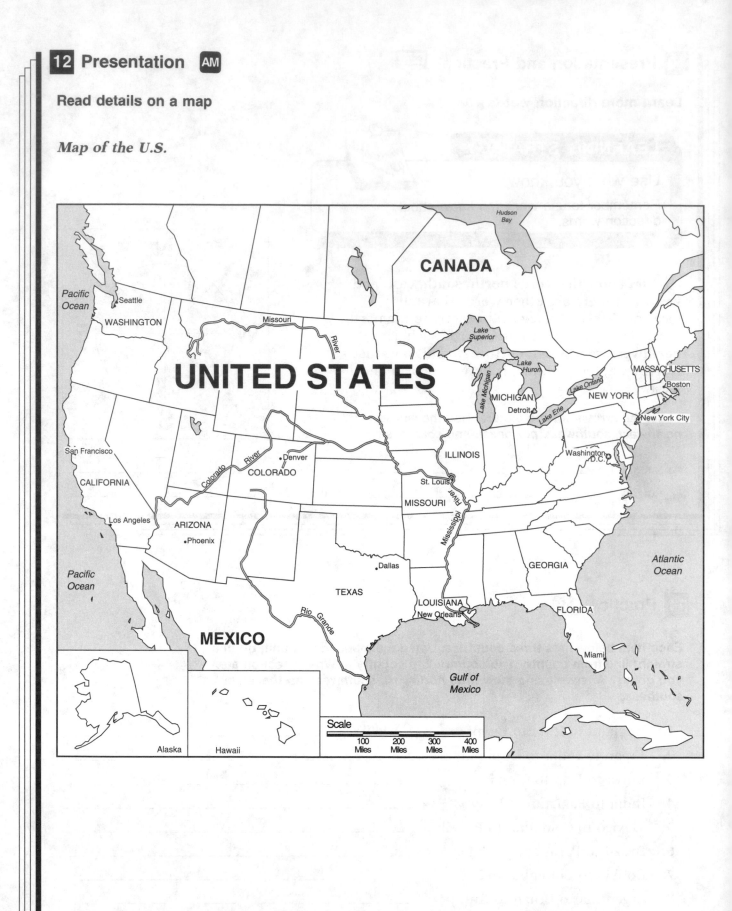

13 Practice AM

Use the map of the U.S. to complete the chart.

	STATE/DISTRICT	CITY	RIVER/LAKE/OCEAN
1.	Massachusetts	*Boston*	*Atlantic Ocean*
2.	_____	Phoenix	_____
3.	_____	_____	Mississippi River
4.	Florida	_____	_____
5.	_____	San Francisco	_____
6.	_____	_____	Lake Michigan
7.	District of Columbia	_____	_____
8.	_____	Seattle	_____
9.	_____	_____	Gulf of Mexico
10.	Colorado	_____	_____

14 Presentation

Measure distances on a map

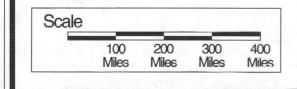

This part of a map is called the **scale.** A scale on a map is used to measure distance on land. This distance ▭ on the map equals 100 miles on land.

15 Practice

Use the U.S. map and its scale. Tell the distance between U.S. cities.

What's the distance between New York City and Washington, D.C.?

New York City

Washington, D.C.

$$\begin{array}{r} 1.25 \\ \times\ 200 \\ \hline 225.00 \end{array}$$

Scale

| 100 Miles | 200 Miles | 300 Miles | 400 Miles |

1. Find a city in the east of the U.S. _____

   Find a city in the west of the U.S. _____

   What is the distance between these two cities? _____

2. Find a city in the north of the U.S. _____

   Find a city in the south. _____

   What is the distance between these two cities? _____

3. Find the distance between other U.S. cities.

   CITY A: _____   DISTANCE: _____

   CITY B: _____

   CITY C: _____   DISTANCE: _____

   CITY D: _____

   CITY E: _____   DISTANCE: _____

   CITY F: _____

16 | Extension

Write about another country

A. Interview a classmate. Write answers to these questions.

1. What country are you from? _____

2. What continent(s) is your country on? _____

3. What countries are near your country? _____

_____

4. Is your country on an ocean? Which ocean? _____

5. What is the name of a river in your country? _____

6. What is an important city in your country? _____

B. Now use your classmate's answers to write a paragraph about your classmate. The paragraph below is a model.

Van is from Cambodia, also called Kampuchea. Cambodia is in Asia, next to Vietnam, Laos, and Thailand. Cambodia is not on an ocean, but the Pacific Ocean and the Indian Ocean are near. The Mekung River is an important river in Van's country. An important city is the capital, Phnom Penh.

MY PARAGRAPH:

_____

_____

_____

_____

_____

_____

_____

UNIT 2: Learning Log

Check what you know. *Review* what you need to know.

VOCABULARY

Map Words
— direction
— east
— map
— north
— northeast
— northwest
— scale
— south
— southeast
— southwest
— west

Place Words
— Central America
— continent
— earth
— lake
— ocean
— river
— world

Continents
— Africa
— Antarctica
— Asia
— Australia
— Europe
— North America
— South America

Oceans
— Arctic Ocean
— Atlantic Ocean
— Indian Ocean
— Pacific Ocean

LEARNING STRATEGIES

I can:
— Use what I know to learn about new information.
— Classify countries by their location.
— Listen selectively and take notes on what I hear.

CONTENT AND LANGUAGE

I can:
— Name the seven continents and four oceans and find them on a map.
— Name countries in North, Central, and South America, and find them on a map.
— Use direction words to talk about the location of a country.
— Write sentences about the location of a country.
— Name countries in Europe, Asia, and Africa, and find them on a map.
— Ask questions and talk about the location of a country.
— Use direction words to talk about traveling from one country to another.
— Name states, cities, and bodies of water in the United States.
— Use a map scale to determine the distance between two U.S. cities.
— Interview a classmate about his/her country.
— Write a paragraph about a country.

SELF-CHECK QUESTIONS

What is interesting in Unit 2? _____
_____
_____

What is easy? _____
_____
_____

What is difficult? _____
_____
_____

How can you learn what is difficult? _____
_____
_____

Nutrition

CONTENT KNOWLEDGE

The Four Basic Food Groups ▪
Healthy diet ▪ Calories ▪ Food
nutrients ▪ Planning meals

LEARNING STRATEGIES

Use what you know ▪ Take
notes ▪ Classify ▪ Listen
selectively ▪ Cooperate

LANGUAGE SKILLS

Because and *too* ▪ adjootivo ▪
Ordinal numbers ▪ Past tense
statements

Preparation

What do you know about food groups?

The Four Basic Food Groups

GROUP 1
BREAD—CEREAL

GROUP 2
MEAT—POULTRY—FISH—BEANS

GROUP 3
MILK

GROUP 4
FRUIT—VEGETABLE

LEARNING STRATEGY

Use what you know

Before you start the unit, think about what you already know about the topic. This gets you ready to learn new information.

A. Think about the foods you eat. Write the names of the foods you ate yesterday.

MORNING

AFTERNOON

EVENING

_____

_____

_____

_____

_____

_____

B. Write the names of five foods you like.

1. _____   2. _____   3. _____

4. _____   5. _____

C. Write five sentences to explain why you don't like or don't eat a type of food very often. Use the adjectives in the box or other adjectives you know.

LANGUAGE SKILL

Use **because** and **too** + *adjective* to explain why you don't like or don't do something.

I don't like french fries **because** they're **too** greasy.
I don't eat chocolate **because** it's **too** fattening.

ADJECTIVE BOX

bitter	expensive	hot	strong
boring	fattening	salty	sweet
cold	greasy	soft	
dry	hard	strange	

1. _____
2. _____
3. _____
4. _____
5. _____

2 Preparation

Interview a classmate

A. Work with a classmate. Find out the foods he or she likes. Write the names of the foods.

FOODS MY CLASSMATE LIKES:

1. _____ 2. _____ 3. _____

   4. _____   5. _____

B. Now find out what foods your classmate doesn't like or doesn't eat and why. Write three complete sentences and use *because* and *too* + adjective to explain your classmate's reasons.

> *Linda doesn't like potato chips because they're too salty.*

FOODS MY CLASSMATE DOESN'T LIKE OR DOESN'T EAT:

1. _____
2. _____
3. _____
4. _____
5. _____

3 Presentation and Practice

Read about taking notes

LEARNING STRATEGY

Take notes

When you're learning new information, a good learning strategy is *taking notes.* The notes help you remember the information. But don't write every word! You don't have time. Just write the most important words.

> YOU HEAR: "Raise your hand to talk."
> To take notes, you write: *Raise hand → talk.*

For each sentence, write the most important words.

1. Cheese is in the Milk food group. _*Cheese: Milk group*_____

2. Chicken is in the Meat–Poultry–Fish–Bean food group. _____

3. Rice is in the Bread–Cereal food group. _____

4. Carrots are a type of vegetable. _____

5. Apples are a type of fruit. _____

6. Hamburger is one kind of meat you can eat. _____

LEARNING STRATEGY

Take notes

Idea Maps are a good way to take notes. When you take notes on an Idea Map, the main idea is in the circle. You write information *about* the main idea on the lines. Write only the most important words.

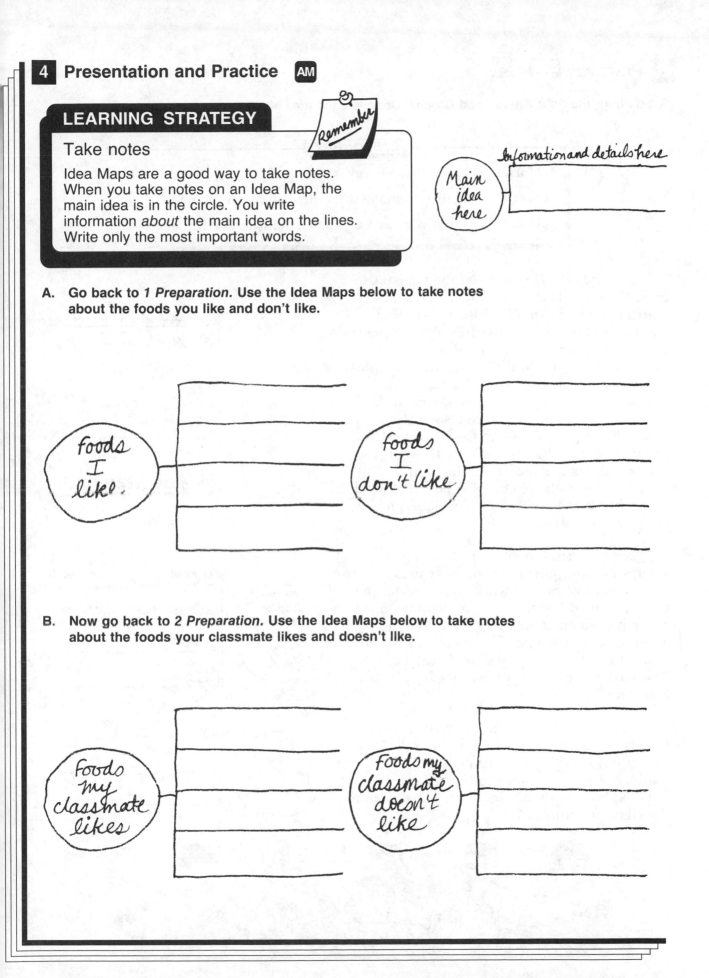

A. Go back to *1 Preparation*. Use the Idea Maps below to take notes about the foods you like and don't like.

B. Now go back to *2 Preparation*. Use the Idea Maps below to take notes about the foods your classmate likes and doesn't like.

5 Practice

Read about the Four Basic Food Groups. Complete the Idea Maps for each paragraph.

WORD BOX	
calorie:	amount of energy in food
energy:	ability to make something move or change
poultry:	birds you can eat, such as chicken or turkey

Your body needs food from the Four Basic Food Groups: (1) Bread–Cereal, (2) Meat–Poultry–Fish–Bean, (3) Milk, and (4) Fruit–Vegetable. Look at the pictures of some foods in the first group shown in *1 Preparation*. Bread, cereal, rice, and tortillas are examples of foods in the Bread–Cereal group. In the second food group are all kinds of meat, fish, poultry, and beans. Eggs are also in the Meat–Poultry–Fish–Bean food group. Milk products are in the third group. Examples of milk products are cheese, butter, and yogurt—and milk, of course. The fourth food group has green and yellow vegetables and all kinds of fruit.

○ 1st - Bread - Cereal
   Meat - Poultry-
   2nd - Fish - Beans

   3rd - Milk

   4th - Fruit - Vegetable

Your body uses foods from these four groups to make energy. Your body uses energy to grow and to work. We measure the energy in food in **calories.** For example, one apple has about 80 calories. Your body uses about 80 calories when you watch TV for an hour. A candy bar has about 270 calories. You have to swim for almost one hour to use 270 calories!

(Body makes energy from food) use energy to grow and work
   calories measure energy
   Ex 1:
   Ex 2:

It's important to eat three meals a day. It's also important to eat foods from the four food groups. And you should eat the right number of calories—not too many and not too few. Your body needs the right foods and the right amounts of food.

(How and what you should eat)

6 Practice

Look at the list of foods you wrote in *1 Preparation*. Did you eat foods from the Four Basic Food Groups? Write a short paragraph about the food you ate from each food group yesterday.

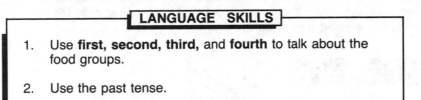

LANGUAGE SKILLS

1. Use **first, second, third,** and **fourth** to talk about the food groups.

2. Use the past tense.

   Yesterday I **ate** bread and rice from the **first** food group.

My Nutrition Yesterday

_____

_____

_____

_____

_____

7 Practice AM

LEARNING STRATEGY

Classify

Classifying (or grouping) things is a good way to organize new information. Classifying helps you learn and remember.

Classify these foods into their food groups.

FOODS TO CLASSIFY

carrots	noodles	bread	grapes	eggs	melon
steak	oatmeal	pineapple	broccoli	yogurt	shrimp
rice	butter	milk	lettuce	tortilla	sausage
watermelon	apple	turkey	cheese	tomato	fish
ice cream	chicken	banana	corn	mushrooms	pork

BREAD—CEREAL	MEAT—POULTRY—FISH—BEANS	MILK		FRUIT—VEGETABLE
				carrots
_____	_____	_____	_____	_____
_____	_____	_____	_____	_____
_____	_____	_____	_____	_____
_____	_____	_____	_____	_____
_____	_____	_____	_____	_____
_____	_____	_____	_____	_____

8 Presentation AM

Take notes about calories

A. You are going to hear about two boys and what they eat for breakfast and lunch. One boy eats food that is good for him. The other eats too much junk food. Listen and complete the chart.

LEARNING STRATEGY

Remember

Listen selectively

Before you listen, look at the chart. What information is missing? Listen for this information.

	VAN'S FOOD	CALORIES	PAUL'S FOOD	CALORIES
BREAKFAST	orange juice	___	bowl of cereal	___
	1 boiled egg	___	_____	150
	1 slice whole wheat bread	___	1 doughnut	125
LUNCH	2 slices chicken	155	_____	290
	_____	152	_____	240
	2 oatmeal cookies	___	candy bar	270
	peach	___	cola	___

B. Now complete these sentences.

1. _____ is eating well.

2. _____ is eating too much junk food.

C. Check your work with a partner.

9 Practice

Now count the calories for Van and Paul. Then answer the questions with short answers.

1. Which boy has more calories at breakfast? *Paul* _____

2. Which boy has more calories at lunch? _____

3. What is the total number of calories in Van's breakfast and lunch? _____

4. What is the total number of calories in Paul's breakfast and lunch? _____

5. Paul is going to eat this for breakfast tomorrow: 1 bowl cereal, 2 glasses milk, 1 slice whole wheat bread, 1 peach. How many calories are in this breakfast? ____

Read about nutrients

Your body needs different materials for good health. These materials are called **nutrients.** Your body needs six kinds of nutrients. These nutrients are in different foods. That is why you should eat foods from the Four Basic Food groups every day. Look at the chart below. The chart lists the six nutrients your body needs and some foods that have a lot of these nutrients.

Nutrients in Foods

NUTRIENT	FOODS WITH A LOT OF THIS NUTRIENT	FOOD GROUP
water	vegetables, fruits, milk, juice	Milk, Fruit–Vegetable
minerals	vegetables, fruits, fish, meat, eggs, milk, cereals	all
carbohydrates	bread, spaghetti, potatoes, rice, cereals	Bread–Cereal, Fruit–Vegetable
fats and oils	cheese, milk, butter, nuts, meat	Meat–Poultry–Fish–Bean, Milk
proteins	meat, eggs, milk, fish, beans, cheese	Meat–Poultry–Fish–Bean, Milk
vitamins	foods from all four groups	all

Most people should eat two or three servings of food from the first three food groups every day, and four to six servings from the fourth food group. This means you should eat two or three servings from the Bread–Cereal group, two or three servings from the Meat–Poultry–Fish–Bean group, two or three servings from the Milk group, and four to six servings from the Fruit–Vegetable group (2–3 fruits and 2–3 vegetables).

But remember—if you eat too much food, it's not good for you. It's important to eat the right foods and the right *amount* of foods!

A. Classify Paul and Van's breakfast and lunch foods. What did Paul and Van eat for breakfast and lunch? Look at the information in *8 Presentation.* Classify each boy's food servings into the Four Basic Food Groups. (One serving = 1 slice bread, 1 cookie, 1 hot dog.)

Number of Servings (Breakfast and Lunch)		
FOOD GROUP	VAN	PAUL
Bread–Cereal		
Meat–Poultry–Fish–Bean		
Milk		
Fruit–Vegetable		

B. Use your chart above and the chart in *10 Presentation* to answer these questions.

1. What nutrients did Van have in his breakfast and lunch?

   _____

2. Which food group is not included in Van's breakfast or lunch?

   _____

3. What nutrients did Paul have in his breakfast and lunch?

   _____

4. Which food group is not included in Paul's breakfast and lunch? _____

   _____

5. What would be a good dinner for Van? _____

   _____

6. What would be a good dinner for Paul? _____

   _____

12 Presentation 📼

Read about calories

ACTIVITY	NUMBER OF CALORIES
Sitting	80–100 an hour
Washing dishes	110–160 an hour
Washing clothes	170–240 an hour
Walking fast	250–350 an hour
Swimming	350+ an hour
Playing tennis	350+ an hour
Dancing	350+ an hour

How many calories are you using? Awake or asleep, you use energy. You get energy from food. Your body uses, or **burns,** calories as energy. When you are active, you use more energy. This means that you burn more calories. When you are not very active, you don't burn many calories. For example, when you are sitting, you are not burning many calories.

We all have to be careful about how much food we eat. Food gives your body the calories it needs to work. But you can eat too much. Then you have more calories than your body needs. Guess what happens then . . .

You can also eat too little food. Then you don't have the calories your body needs. Can you guess what happens then?

13 Practice

Answer the questions with complete sentences.

1. Sally takes in about 1800 calories a day. She watches television a lot and she doesn't like sports. Sally burns about 1200 calories a day. What's going to happen to Sally? ___*She's going to gain weight.*___

2. David goes to school during the day and cleans offices at night. He works very hard. He's also on the school soccer team. He burns about 3000 calories a day. He eats well, but he doesn't eat a lot. He takes in about 2000 calories a day. What's going to happen to David? _____

3. Look at Paul's lunch in *8 Presentation*. To burn the calories he ate at lunch, about how long does he have to sit? _____

    About how long does he have to swim? _____

4. Look at Van's lunch in *8 Presentation*. To burn the calories he ate at lunch, about how long does he have to wash dishes? _____

    About how long does he have to play tennis? _____

Planning meals

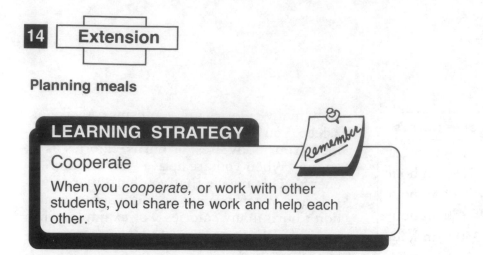

LEARNING STRATEGY

Cooperate

When you *cooperate*, or work with other students, you share the work and help each other.

Work with two classmates. Plan your own meals for one day. Write what you are going to eat for breakfast, lunch, and dinner. Include 2–3 servings from each of the first three food groups, and 4–6 servings from the Fruit–Vegetable group. Total calories for the day have to be 2500 or less! Use the foods in the chart below and other foods from this unit.

BREAD—CEREAL	CALORIES	MILK	CALORIES
rice (1/2 cup)	110	cheese (1 slice)	105
hamburger bun	109	ice cream (1/2 cup)	140
cornflakes	85	yogurt (1 cup)	150
oatmeal cookies (2)	120	milk (1 glass)	159
MEAT—POULTRY—FISH—BEAN		**FRUIT—VEGETABLE**	
fish sticks (4)	160	orange	70
shrimp (3 oz.)	100	pear	100
hamburger (3 oz.)	245	grapes (1 cup)	106
bacon (2 slices)	100	corn (1/2 cup)	60
pork chop (3 oz.)	320	potato (baked)	92
steak (3 oz.)	400	spinach (1 cup)	45
chicken (3 oz.)	100	carrots (1 cup)	50
egg (boiled)	81	lettuce (3 leaves)	6
baked beans (1/2 cup)	150		

BREAKFAST

_____

_____

_____

_____

_____

_____

_____

LUNCH

_____

_____

_____

_____

_____

_____

_____

DINNER

_____

_____

_____

_____

_____

_____

_____

UNIT 3: Learning Log

Check what you know. *Review* what you need to learn.

VOCABULARY

Food Groups
— Bread–Cereal
— Meat–Poultry–Fish–Beans
— Milk
— Fruit–Vegetable

Adjectives
— bitter
— boring
— cold
— dry
— expensive
— fattening
— greasy
— hard
— hot
— salty
— soft
— strange
— strong
— sweet

Colors
— green
— yellow

Foods
— apples
— bacon
— bagel
— banana
— beans
— bread
— broccoli
— butter
— candy
— carrots
— cereal
— cheese
— chicken

— cola
— corn
— cornflakes
— doughnut
— eggs
— fish
— french fries
— fruit
— grapes
— hamburger
— ice cream
— juice
— lettuce
— meat
— melon
— milk
— mushrooms
— noodles
— nuts
— oatmeal
— orange
— peach
— pear
— pineapple
— pork
— potato
— poultry
— rice
— sausage
— shrimp
— spaghetti
— spinach
— steak
— tomato
— tortilla
— turkey
— vegetable
— watermelon
— yogurt

Useful Verbs
— eat
— like
— raise

Ordinal Numbers
— first
— second
— third
— fourth

Food-related Words
— active
— bowl
— breakfast
— burn
— calorie
— carbohydrates
— dinner
— energy
— fats
— glass
— lunch
— minerals
— nutrients
— nutrition
— oils
— product
— protein
— serving
— slice
— vitamin

LEARNING STRATEGIES

I can:

—— Use what I know to understand new information.
—— Take notes.
—— Take notes on Idea Maps.
—— Classify.
—— Listen selectively.
—— Cooperate with my classmates.

CONTENT AND LANGUAGE

I can:

—— Identify foods in the Four Basic Food Groups.
—— Write the names of foods.
—— Use **because** and **too** + *adjective* to explain why I don't like or don't do something.
—— Read and take notes about food and food groups.
—— Use ordinal numbers in sentences.
—— Classify foods into the Four Basic Food Groups.
—— Listen to information about calories in foods.
—— Add calories of different foods to get the total calories for a meal.
—— Read and answer questions about nutrients.
—— Read and answer questions about calories.
—— Plan meals for breakfast, lunch, and dinner that have the Four Basic Food Groups.

SELF-CHECK QUESTIONS

What is interesting in Unit 3? _____

_____

_____

What is easy? _____

_____

_____

What is difficult? _____

_____

_____

How can you learn what is difficult? _____

_____

_____

Literature: A Fable

UNIT 4

CONTENT KNOWLEDGE

Literary analysis: Setting, characters, events, moral

LEARNING STRATEGIES

Use what you know ▪ Listen selectively ▪ Make predictions ▪ Take notes ▪ Summarize

LANGUAGE SKILLS

Past tense ▪ Adjectives

1 Preparation

What do you already know?

A Fable: The Lion and the Mouse

Write three things you know about lions. Write three things you know about mice.

LION

1. _A lion likes to sleep in the sun._
2. _____
3. _____
4. _____

MOUSE

1. _A mouse can run fast._
2. _____
3. _____
4. _____

2 Preparation

What is going to happen?

**Look at the picture of the Lion and the Mouse. Work with a partner. Write
how you think the story begins. Some words are suggested in the Word Box.**

LANGUAGE SKILL

Use the past tense and the past continuous to tell stories.

The Mouse **ran** fast. = past tense
The Lion **was sleeping.** = past continuous

WORD BOX

little	was sleeping	breakfast	mouse
brave	lion	jumped	sun
one day	woke up	ran	food
teeth	terrible	great	kept sleeping
face	hungry	scared	laughed

_____
_____
_____
_____
_____

Listen and take notes

A.   Listen to the beginning of the story. Take notes below by circling the words you hear.

> **LEARNING STRATEGY**
>
> *Remember*
>
> **Listen selectively**
> Don't forget to look at the words *before* you
> listen. Then you know what words to listen for.

1.   The day was . . .   dark / windy / (sunny) / cool / (warm)
2.   The Lion was . . .   next to the lake / in the tall grass /
                                 under a tree / in a tree / in the shade
3.   The Lion felt . . .   happy / tired / calm / content / angry
4.   Suddenly, he felt . . .   hungry / sleepy / nervous / warm / full
5.   His head was . . .   magnificent / heavy / furry / blond
6.   Soon, he . . .   ate breakfast / yawned / closed his eyes /
                                 saw a Mouse / was sleeping / was dreaming
7.   Then he felt . . .   rain / angry / a Mouse / scared / sleepy
8.   He saw . . .   rain / two eyes / his breakfast was gone
9.   He . . .   shared his breakfast / roared / jumped up /
                                 grabbed the Mouse / ate the Mouse / laughed

B.   Check your work with a classmate.

---

4 Practice AM

**Are the statements below true or false? If you think a statement is false,
make it a true statement.**

1.   _____false_____   The Lion fell asleep ~~under a tree~~. *in the sun*

2.   _____   The Lion lay down to eat breakfast.

3.   _____   The Mouse ran across the Lion's paw.

4.   _____   For a moment, the Lion thought it was raining.

5.   _____   The Lion saw the Mouse's ears first.

6.   _____   The Mouse was standing on the Lion's back.

7.   _____   The Lion was angry at the Mouse.

8.   _____   The Mouse was white.

9.   _____   The Lion was ready to eat the Mouse.

How to analyze stories

When we read and talk about stories, we look at certain parts of the story. *Where* does the story take place? That's called the **setting.** The setting of a story can be a house, a town, the countryside, a city. The setting can be warm or cool, sunny or rainy, beautiful or ugly.

Who is the story about? Those are the **characters.** A story's characters can be people, such as a king, a doctor, or a teenager. A character can also be an animal with an interesting story to tell, or sometimes even a plant!

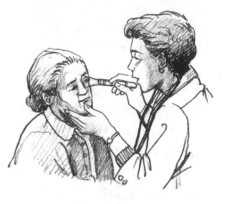

What happens in the story? This is called the **plot.** The plot is made up of **events,** what happens first, second, third, and so on. Events can be when a house burns, when a bad storm comes, when two characters get married, or when a character gets a new job.

The setting, the characters, and the plot, with all its events, are important parts of a story.

6 **Practice**

A. **The sentences on the left describe parts of a story. Match each sentence to the part it describes (a–d, listed on the right). You can use a part more than once.**

1. __*c*__ one thing that happens in the story   **a.** Setting

2. ____ where the story takes place   **b.** Character

3. ____ the main person in the story   **c.** Event

4. ____ all of the events in the story   **d.** Plot

5. ____ an important thing that happens to a person

6. ____ an important friend in the story

B. **Now imagine that a movie was made of the story of *your* life. Answer the questions below in 1–2 sentences. Use complete sentences.**

1. The movie starts with where you are at this moment. Describe your setting.

   _____

   _____

2. You are the main character in the movie. Describe yourself. What do you look like? What is your personality like?

   _____

   _____

3. Who are some other characters in the movie about your life? Describe them.

   _____

   _____

4. The movie needs to show some events in your life. What are two important events the movie should show?

   _____

   _____

7 Practice

Answer these questions about *The Lion and the Mouse.* Use complete sentences. Some words are suggested in the Adjective Box. You can also look back in the unit if you need to.

ADJECTIVE BOX

rainy	cold	small	beautiful	big
grassy	angry	mountainous	smart	kingly
brown	warm	magnificent	sunny	breezy

LANGUAGE SKILL

Use adjectives to describe people, places, and things.

---

1. Describe the setting of the story. *It's a warm and sunny day.* _____

2. Who are the characters in *The Lion and the Mouse?*

   _____

3. Describe what the Lion looks like. _____

   _____

4. What does the Mouse look like? _____

8 Practice

LEARNING STRATEGY

Make predictions

When you read, it's important to think ahead and *make predictions.* What's going to happen next? Use your imagination. It makes reading more fun!

The Lion has the Mouse! How's the Mouse going to get away? I'll bet the Mouse *bites* the Lion . . . and runs!

A. Look at your guess in *2 Preparation*, page 42. Were you right about the beginning of the story?

B. Look at the picture below. Work with a partner. Write three sentences about what is going to happen next. Use the past tense—and your imagination!

_____

_____

_____

_____

_____

_____

9 Presentation

Read more about the Lion and the Mouse

Think about your guess as you read. Were you right? If not, what is happening instead?

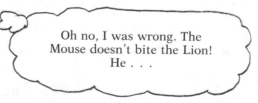

Oh no, I was wrong. The Mouse doesn't bite the Lion! He . . .

"Brown mouse for breakfast!" roared the Lion. "I love brown mice!"
"Oh, please don't eat me!" begged the Mouse. He was very scared, but his mind was working fast. "If you let me live, I can help you some day. Let me go, I beg you, and I'll never forget your kindness."

Read about Story Maps

Below is a Story Map. You can use a Story Map to take notes on fictional stories. Look at the Story Map. Then read about the parts of the Story Map and what information goes in each part.

A Story Map

Time of day: _____

Setting: [_____]

Characters: _____ _____
_____ _____

Problem: [_____]

Plot: {
Event 1: _____
Event 2: _____
Event 3: _____
Event 4: _____
Event 5: _____
Event 6: _____
Event 7: _____
Event 8: _____
}

Moral: [_____]

The Time of Day: When does the story happen? Morning, noon, night?

The Setting: Where does the story happen? In a city, the country, a house? Is it a nice day, or cold and rainy?

Characters: Who is the story about? A teenager, a king, a mechanic? A person, an animal, a plant? What do the characters look like?

Problem: In fiction, as in real life, there is usually some problem to be solved. The problem is usually not easy to solve. The characters have to think, and work, and try hard to solve the problem.

Events: What happens in the story? The main things that happen are the events. Events can be sad, happy, exciting, scary, terrible, or wonderful.

Moral: Fictional stories make a point, or have a lesson for you to learn. This lesson—the main idea the writer wants you to learn—is called the moral. Some morals are: "Money doesn't buy you happiness" and "Learn from your experiences."

11 Practice AM

A. As you know, Story Maps have many parts. Match each part below to its definition.

1. __d__ the trouble in the story; what needs to be solved   **a.** Event
2. ____ the people in the story   **b.** Moral
3. ____ when the story takes place   **c.** Setting
4. ____ something that happens in the story   **d.** Problem
5. ____ where the story takes place   **e.** Characters
6. ____ the main point or lesson of the story   **f.** Time of day

B. Now match these pictures to the parts of the Story Map, using a–f above.

1. __e__

2. ____

3. ____

4. ____

5. ____

You've read part of *The Lion and the Mouse.* Use the Story Map below to take notes on what you know about the story. Problem 1 and Events 1–4 are filled in as examples.

LEARNING STRATEGY

Remember

Take notes

Taking notes helps you organize information. You can also use your notes to review information later!

Fill in the parts *Time of Day, Setting,* and *Characters.* (Look back to *3* and *9 Presentation* for help.) You will fill in the rest of the Story Map as you read more of the story.

A Story Map

Time of day: _____

Setting:

Characters: _____

_____

Problem:
1. The Mouse wants to get free from the Lion.
2.

Plot:
Event 1: The Lion fell asleep.
Event 2: The Mouse ran on his face.
Event 3: The Lion caught the Mouse.
Event 4: The Mouse begged to be let go.
Event 5: _____
Event 6: _____
Event 7: _____
Event 8: _____

Moral:

13 Presentation 🔲

The story continues

The Lion smiled. What a silly idea! A tiny brown mouse help *him*, the King of all animals? The Lion laughed. Yes, the idea was funny. He decided to let the Mouse go. He opened his paw—and off the Mouse ran!

The Lion, feeling merciful and grand, went for a walk. He was holding his head so high, he didn't see the trap. The ropes fell over him, and he couldn't move. He was trapped! *Oh!* he roared. He yelled so loud, all the animals heard him. Even the Mouse heard him.

14 Practice

LEARNING STRATEGY

Write a summary

When you write a *summary*, you write the most important idea. If you can write a summary, then you understand what's happening in the story.

A. Look at the Story Map on page 49. The four Events that are filled in are summaries. The Problem that is filled in is also a summary. Two more events just happened in the story. Write in Event 5 and Event 6 in your Story Map. In one sentence each, write summaries of what just happened in the story.

B. Write a summary of the Lion's problem. Write one sentence under Problem to describe the Lion's trouble.

15 Presentation and Practice 📼

Listen, take notes, and write a summary

A. Look at the four pictures below. Then listen. Which picture describes what happens in the story? Write the letter. _____

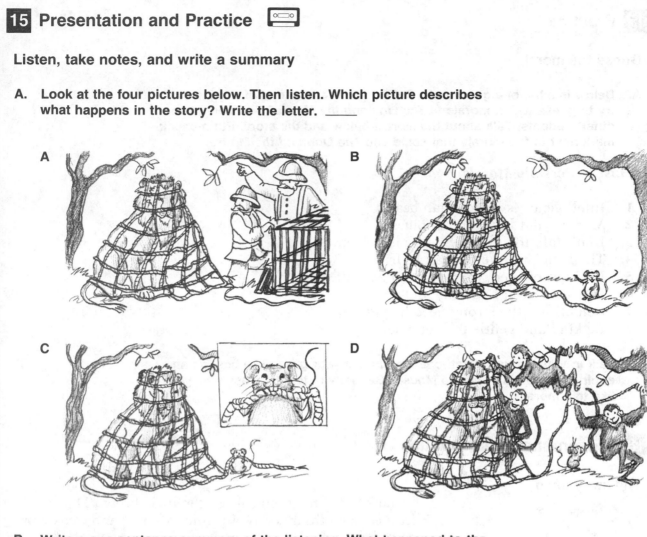

A

B

C

D

B. Write a one-sentence summary of the listening. What happened to the Lion? Add this sentence to your Story Map as Event 7.

16 Presentation 📼

What's a fable?

There are many stories like *The Lion and the Mouse.* This type of story is called a **fable.** A fable tries to teach you something. As you know, the lesson of the fable, or its main idea, is called the **moral.** The moral is the idea the author wants you to learn. Usually, the moral of a fable is the last sentence in the story.

Aesop is the author of this fable. Aesop was Greek and lived about 620–560 B.C. He never wrote these fables down on paper. He was a great storyteller, and he told these fables to other people. These people told others, and so the fables were not forgotten. Eventually some people wrote the fables, and so today we can read them.

17 Practice

Guess the moral

A. Below is a list of eight morals. Before you read the end of the story, try to guess which morals fit *The Lion and the Mouse?* Work with two other students. Talk about the morals below and the story. Put a check mark next to the morals that could end *The Lion and the Mouse.*

A List of Possible Morals

1. Intelligence is better than beauty.
2. Money can't buy you happiness.
3. Don't talk too much. Silence is golden.
4. The little and the big can be friends.
5. In times of need, the weak can help the strong.
6. Be careful what you say and do.
7. Sometimes the strong need help, too.
8. Be kind and gentle to everyone.

B. Talk in your group. Which *one* moral does your group like best as an ending to *The Lion and the Mouse?* Be ready to tell the class why you like this moral.

18 Presentation and Practice

The story ends

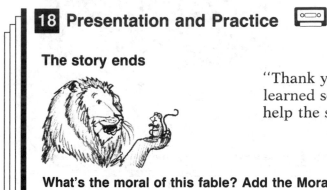

"Thank you," the Lion said to the little brown Mouse. "I learned something today. In times of need, the weak can help the strong."

What's the moral of this fable? Add the Moral to your Story Map, page 49.

19 Extension

Re-tell the story and write your own moral

Are you surprised at the moral that ends this fable? Can you think of a better or different moral for this story?

A. Work with two other students. Re-tell the story in your own words, using complete sentences. Then write a different moral to end this story. State the moral in one sentence.

B. Read what you have written to the class and say why your moral fits this story.

UNIT 4: Learning Log

Check what you know. *Review* what you need to learn.

VOCABULARY

Story Analysis
— characters
— events
— fable
— moral
— plot
— problem
— setting
— Story Map
— time of day

Adjectives
— brave
— breezy
— brown
— calm
— content
— funny
— grassy
— great
— heavy
— hungry
— little
— magnificent
— scared
— sharp
— small
— smart
— sunny
— terrible
— tiny

Other
— breakfast
— eyes
— face
— food
— kindness
— lion
— mouse
— movie
— ropes
— storyteller
— sun
— teeth
— trap

Verbs
— bite
— fall
— gnaw
— jump
— laugh
— roar
— run
— sleep
— wake up
— yawn

CONTENT AND LANGUAGE

I can:
— Say if a statement is true or false, and correct statements that are false.
— Read and answer questions about how we analyze stories.
— Identify and describe the setting of a story.
— Identify and describe the characters of a story.
— Identify and describe the events of a story.
— Identify and describe the problems in a story.
— Make a summary of the events and problems in a story.
— Talk about morals of a story.
— Identify the moral of a story.
  Re-tell a story in my own words.
— Make a Story Map of a story.

SELF-CHECK QUESTIONS

What is interesting in Unit 4? _____

_____

_____

What is easy? _____

_____

_____

What is difficult? _____

_____

_____

How can you learn what is difficult? _____

_____

_____

LEARNING STRATEGIES

I can:
— Use what I know to understand new information.
— Listen selectively and take notes on what I hear.
— Make a prediction about what is going to happen in a story.
— Check to see if my prediction was correct.
— Take notes on a Story Map.
— Make a summary of information.

Math: Multiplication and Division

UNIT 5

CONTENT KNOWLEDGE

Reviewing addition and subtraction · Listening to numbers · Multiplication and division · Averages · Solving word problems · Geometric shapes · Area

LEARNING STRATEGIES

Use what you know · Make a picture · Cooperate · Read selectively · Listen selectively

MATH STRATEGIES

Make a table · Use Problem Solving steps

LANGUAGE SKILLS

Past tense statements and questions · Simple present statements and questions · *How many* · *How much*

1 Preparation

What do you know about multiplication and division?

$4 \times 6 = 24$
$24 \div 6 = 4$

LEARNING STRATEGY

Remember

Use what you know

Before you start a lesson, think. What do you already know about a topic? *Using what you know* helps you learn.

Read the words in the Word Box. Then write the words that go with each operation.

WORD BOX

difference	factor	dividend	times
quotient	total	less	addend
product	divisor	greater than	sum

ADDITION	SUBTRACTION	MULTIPLICATION	DIVISION
_____	_____	_____	_____
_____	_____	_____	_____
_____	_____	_____	_____

2 Presentation 📼

Multiplication

Mr. Rodríguez showed his class how lima bean seeds grow in jars. He had 3 jars and he put 2 seeds in each jar.

How many seeds did Mr. Rodríguez put in all the jars?

A. One way to solve this problem is to **add.** You can add to find how many seeds are in the jars.

$2 + 2 + 2 = 6$

B. Another way to solve the problem is to **make a picture** or **a table.**

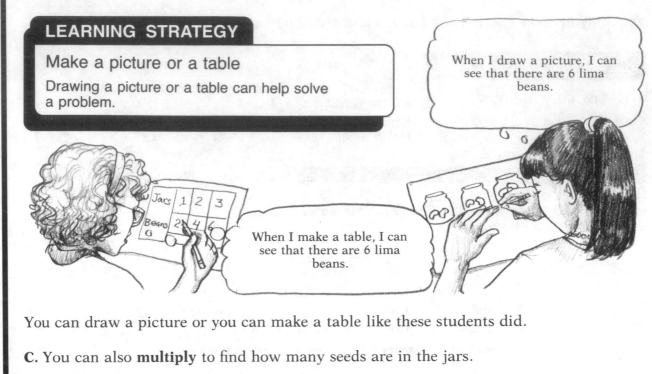

LEARNING STRATEGY

Make a picture or a table
Drawing a picture or a table can help solve
a problem.

When I draw a picture, I can see that there are 6 lima beans.

When I make a table, I can see that there are 6 lima beans.

You can draw a picture or you can make a table like these students did.

C. You can also **multiply** to find how many seeds are in the jars.

$$3 \text{ twos} = 6$$
$$3 \times 2 = 6 \quad \text{OR} \quad \begin{array}{r} 3 \\ \times 2 \\ \hline 6 \end{array}$$

Mr. Rodríguez had 6 lima beans in the jars.

We read the equation (or number sentence) $3 \times 2 = 6$ as, "Three times two equals six." We can also say, "The product of three times two is six." Three and two are **factors.** Six is the **product.** The product is the result of a multiplication.

3 Practice

A. Write the product. Then write the words for each number sentence. Use two ways to write the words as shown in the examples. If you do not know the product, use addition, draw a picture, or make a table.

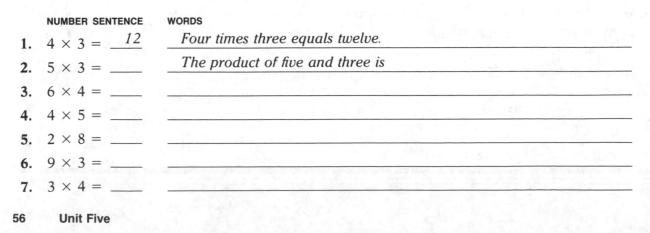

	NUMBER SENTENCE	WORDS
1.	$4 \times 3 = \underline{\quad 12 \quad}$	*Four times three equals twelve.*
2.	$5 \times 3 = \underline{\quad\quad}$	*The product of five and three is*
3.	$6 \times 4 = \underline{\quad\quad}$	
4.	$4 \times 5 = \underline{\quad\quad}$	
5.	$2 \times 8 = \underline{\quad\quad}$	
6.	$9 \times 3 = \underline{\quad\quad}$	
7.	$3 \times 4 = \underline{\quad\quad}$	

8. 7 × 4 = ____ ______________________________

9. 1 × 1 = ____ ______________________________

10. 6 × 2 = ____ ______________________________

B. Check your work with a partner. Then take turns reading the number sentences aloud. Compare: When you did not know the product, did you and your partner use the same approach? Did you add? Make a picture? Make a table?

LEARNING STRATEGY

Cooperate

Checking your work with a partner helps you both learn.

4 Presentation and Practice AM

Multiplication Table

One way to multiply one-digit numbers is by using a **Multiplication Table.** The Multiplication Table shows all the products for the numbers 1 through 9.

Use the example shown earlier:

Mr. Rodríguez put 2 lima bean seeds in each of 3 jars.
How many lima bean seeds did he put in all the jars?

Look at the Multiplication Table. Note the column for 3 jars and the row for 2 lima bean seeds in each jar. There are 6 lima bean seeds in all the jars.

Fill in the missing numbers on the table.

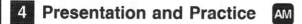

Multiplication Table

LIMA BEANS IN EACH JAR	(JARS) SETS OF LIMA BEANS 1	2	3	4	5	6	7	8	9	10
1	1	2	___	4	___	6	7	___	9	10
2	___	4	6	___	___	12	14	16	___	20
3	3	___	9	12	15	___	___	24	27	___
4	___	8	___	16	20	24	28	___	36	40
5	5	10	15	___	25	30	35	___	45	___
6	___	12	18	___	___	36	___	48	___	60
7	7	___	___	28	35	42	___	56	63	70
8	8	16	___	32	40	___	___	64	72	___
9	9	18	27	36	45	54	63	72	81	90

Division

Mr. Rodríguez had 12 seeds. He wanted to give each of 4 students a jar with an equal number of seeds. How many seeds were in each jar?

A. One way to solve this problem is to make a multiplication problem and draw a picture, like the following:

$$\underline{\quad?\quad} \times 4 = 12$$

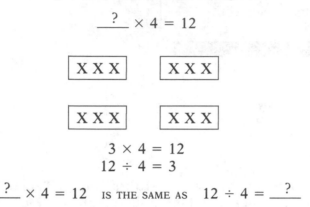

$$3 \times 4 = 12$$
$$12 \div 4 = 3$$

$$\underline{\quad?\quad} \times 4 = 12 \quad \text{IS THE SAME AS} \quad 12 \div 4 = \underline{\quad?\quad}$$

B. Another way to solve the problem is to use the Multiplication Table. Part of the table is shown below. Find the column that shows 4 jars. Then find the place that shows 12 lima bean seeds. Read across to the left to see how many lima beans are in each jar. There are 3 lima bean seeds in each jar.

Multiplication Table

LIMA BEANS IN EACH JAR	JARS (SETS OF LIMA BEANS)			
	1	**2**	**3**	**4**
1	1	2	—	4
2	—	4	6	—
3	3	—	9	12

C. The equation $12 \div 4 = 3$ is the same as: $\dfrac{12}{4} = 3$ AND $4\overline{)12}^{\,3}$

We read the equation (or number sentence) $12 \div 4 = 3$ as "Twelve divided by four equals three." In this equation, 12 is the **dividend;** 4 is the **divisor;** and 3 is the **quotient.** Other ways of showing this are:

$$\frac{\text{dividend}}{\text{divisor}} = \text{quotient} \quad \text{AND} \quad \text{divisor}\overline{)\text{dividend}}^{\,\text{quotient}}$$

6 Practice

A. Write the answer. Then write the words for each number sentence.

	NUMBER SENTENCE	WORDS
1.	36 ÷ 6 = __6__	*Thirty-six divided by six is six.*
2.	27 ÷ 3 = ____	
3.	26 ÷ 2 = ____	
4.	24 ÷ 8 = ____	
5.	42 ÷ 7 = ____	
6.	45 ÷ 9 = ____	
7.	18 ÷ 2 = ____	
8.	45 ÷ 5 = ____	
9.	44 ÷ 4 = ____	
10.	12 ÷ 1 = ____	

B. Check your work with a partner. Then take turns reading the number sentences aloud.

C. Now take turns identifying the dividend, divisor, and quotient.

7 Practice

LEARNING STRATEGY

Read selectively

Find the word in each sentence that shows the operation. This helps solve the problem.

Remember

"Twelve times two is ___."
Hmm. *Times* means to multiply.

A. Write the answer to each problem. Then write the number sentence.

	PROBLEM	NUMBER SENTENCE
1.	Twelve times two is _twenty-four._	12 × 2 = 24
2.	The quotient of fourteen divided by seven is _____	_____
3.	Twenty-four divided by six is _____	_____
4.	Twenty-one divided by seven is _____	_____
5.	The product of eight and nine is _____	_____
6.	Fifty-six divided by eight is _____	_____
7.	Nine times three is _____	_____
8.	The product of six and five is _____	_____
9.	The quotient of twelve divided by one is _____	_____
10.	Four times three is _____	_____

B. Check your work with a partner. Then take turns reading the number sentences aloud.

A. **Solve the problems. Then write the words for each problem.**

PROBLEM   WORDS

1. $12 + 7 =$ _19_   *Twelve plus seven is nineteen.*

2. $48 \div 8 =$ ____

3. $12 \times 4 =$ ____

4. $15 - 8 =$ ____

5. $36 - 6 =$ ____

6. $49 \div 7 =$ ____

7. $8 + 18 =$ ____

8. $8 \times 9 =$ ____

9. $11 - 9 =$ ____

10.
$$\begin{array}{r} 13 \\ -\ 8 \\ \hline \end{array}$$

11.
$$\begin{array}{r} 7 \\ \times 6 \\ \hline \end{array}$$

12.
$$\begin{array}{r} 15 \\ +12 \\ \hline \end{array}$$

13. $8\overline{)64}$

14.
$$\begin{array}{r} 14 \\ +16 \\ \hline \end{array}$$

15. $4\overline{)28}$

B. **Check your work with a partner. Then take turns reading the number sentences aloud.**

9 Presentation

Solving word problems

1. Understand the QUESTION.
2. Find the DATA.
3. Choose the OPERATION.
4. Find the ANSWER.
5. CHECK back.

Paul wanted to find the number of calories in his breakfast and lunch on school days. The total number of calories Paul ate each day for breakfast and lunch was 622, 650, 600, 750, and 725. How many calories did Paul eat in all five days?

1. Understand the QUESTION.

   (HINT: Rewrite the question as a statement)

   The number of calories Paul ate was _____ .

2. Find the DATA.

   The calories for each of the five days were:
   622, 650, 600, 750, and 725

3. Choose the OPERATION.

   The question asks for the number of calories Paul ate in all five days.
   We should add.

4. Find the ANSWER.

   (HINT: First add each
   column *down*.)

   $$\begin{array}{r} 622 \\ 650 \\ 600 \\ 750 \\ +725 \\ \hline 3347 \end{array}$$

5. CHECK back.

   Read the question again. Make sure you understand the question correctly.
   Are you using the right operation? This time, add all columns *up*, not down.
   You can also use a calculator to check your work.

   The number of calories Paul ate was 3347.

Solve the problems. Use the five Problem Solving steps.

1. How many calories did Van eat at breakfast and lunch during the week?

DAY	CALORIES
Monday	1214
Tuesday	987
Wednesday	1020
Thursday	1138
Friday	1095

    1. QUESTION   _Van ate _____ calories for breakfast and lunch during the week._

    2. DATA   _1214, 987, 1020, 1138, 1095_

    3. OPERATION   _addition_

    4. ANSWER
        $$\begin{array}{r} 1214 \\ 987 \\ 1020 \\ 1138 \\ +1095 \\ \hline 5454 \end{array}$$

    5. CHECK   Read the question again. Are you using the right operation? Now add the numbers in a different direction.

        Van ate 5454 calories for breakfast and lunch during the week.

2. Van ate more calories than Paul. How many more? (See 9 Presentation for Paul's calories.)

    1. QUESTION   _____

    2. DATA   _____

    3. OPERATION   _____

    4. ANSWER

    5. CHECK   _____

3. Roberto had one hot dog, a hot dog bun, milk, and some fruit for lunch on Monday, Tuesday, Wednesday, Thursday, and Friday. There were about 700 calories in his lunch each day. How many calories did he eat all week?

    1. QUESTION   _____

    2. DATA   _____

    3. OPERATION   _____

    4. ANSWER

    5. CHECK   _____

4. María ate exactly the same breakfast each day during the week. She ate 400 calories on Monday. How many calories did she eat all 7 days during the week?

1. QUESTION _____

2. DATA _____

3. OPERATION _____

4. ANSWER

5. CHECK _____

5. Paul ate about 2500 calories on Monday and 2200 calories on Tuesday. How many more calories did he eat on Monday than he did on Tuesday?

1. QUESTION _____

2. DATA _____

3. OPERATION _____

4. ANSWER

5. CHECK _____

6. Paul ate 2800 calories on Tuesday and Van ate 2200 calories. How many calories did they eat in all?

1. QUESTION _____

2. DATA _____

3. OPERATION _____

4. ANSWER

5. CHECK _____

7. Lin used a chart to find out how many calories she ate at each meal on Friday.

MEAL	FOOD	CALORIES
BREAKFAST	orange juice 1 fried egg 1 slice white bread	87 108 60
LUNCH	1 slice chicken peach skim milk	77 40 90
DINNER	veal chop broccoli mashed potatoes yogurt	185 40 120 150

How many calories did she eat at breakfast?

1. QUESTION _____

2. DATA _____

3. OPERATION _____

4. ANSWER

5. CHECK _____

8. How many calories did Lin eat at dinner?

1. QUESTION _____

2. DATA _____

3. OPERATION _____

4. ANSWER

5. CHECK _____

11 Presentation

Finding averages

Ms. Delgado collected information about the rainfall in Santa Fe, New Mexico. In one year, the rainfall was 9 inches. The next year it was 11 inches, and the next year it was 7 inches. What was the average rainfall over the three years?

To find the average of three numbers, add the numbers and divide by 3.

   a. $9 + 11 + 7 = 27$ **b.** $27 \div 3 = 9$ **c.** The average rainfall in Santa Fe over the three years was 9 inches.

Other examples:

1. Find the average distance of 12 miles, 8 miles, 14 miles, and 6 miles.
   a. $12 + 8 + 14 + 6 = 40$ **b.** $40 \div 4 = 10$ **c.** The average distance is 10 miles.

2. There is one bean plant in each of five jars. After two weeks the heights of the plants are: 5 inches, 4 inches, 6 inches, 7 inches, and 3 inches. Find the average height of the plants.
   a. $5 + 4 + 6 + 7 + 3 = 25$ **b.** $25 \div 5 = 5$ **c.** The average height of the plants is 5 inches.

3. Find the average of 14, 12, and 10:
   a. $14 + 12 + 10 = 36$ **b.** $36 \div 3 = 12$ **c.** The average is 12.

12 Practice

Find the averages of the numbers in the word problems.

1. What is the average distance of 12 miles, 18 miles, 22 miles, and 8 miles? _____

2. Find the average height of 5 plants with the following heights: 7 inches, 11 inches, 15 inches, 18 inches, and 24 inches. _____

3. What is the average of 31, 28, and 7? _____

4. What is the average weight of 4 rocks that weigh 25 grams, 14 grams, 11 grams, and 18 grams? _____

5. The three deepest oceans of the world are the Pacific Ocean (about 11 miles), the Atlantic Ocean (about 8 miles), and the Indian Ocean (about 8 miles). What is their approximate average depth?

_____

6. The temperatures in four cities were as follows: Chicago 33°F, Washington, D.C., 42°F, Boston 18°F, and Minneapolis 11°F. What was the average temperature of these four cities?

_____

7. Juan worked 8 hours and made $43, while María worked half as long and made $24. What was the average amount of money María made per hour?

_____

8. The weights of 5 balls used in different sports are as follows: baseball–5 ounces; basketball–22 ounces; football–15 ounces; soccer–16 ounces; and tennis–2 ounces. What is the average weight of the balls?

_____

13 Preparation

Geometric shapes

Write the correct name under each geometric shape.

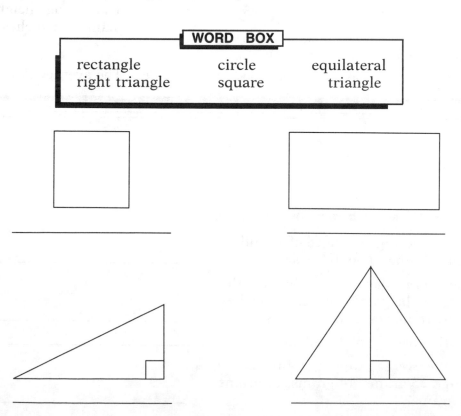

WORD BOX
rectangle   circle   equilateral
right triangle   square   triangle

_____

_____

_____

_____

14 Presentation

Using multiplication to find the area

A. How much area is covered by the rectangle? You can find the area by adding the small squares. You can also find the area with multiplication.

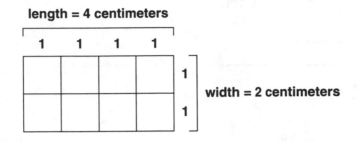

By addition, the area is $1 + 1 + 1 + 1 + 1 + 1 + 1 + 1 = 8$ square centimeters.

By multiplication, the area is the **length times** the **width,** or $4 \times 2 = 8$ square centimeters.

B. You can also find the area of a square with multiplication.

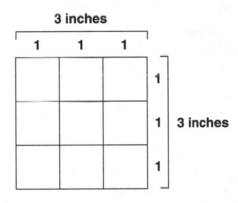

The area of this square is $3 \times 3 = 9$ sq. inches.

C. The area of a right triangle is ½ the **base times** the **height.**

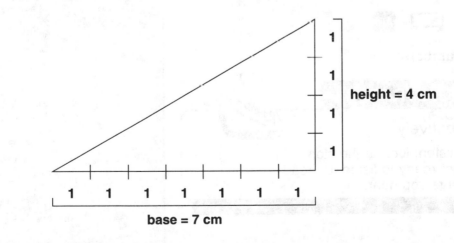

The area of this right triangle is $½ \times 7 \times 4 = 14$ sq cm.

15 Practice AM

Find the area of each figure. Write the area on the line below the figure.

12 cm

6 cm

1. _____

8 cm

5 cm

2. _____

8 in.

8 in.

3. _____

7 cm

6 cm

4. _____

7 cm

4 cm

5. _____

9 in.

8 in.

6. _____

8 cm

4 cm   6 cm

7. _____

6 in

2 in.   5 in.

8. _____

16 Practice AM

Listening to numbers

LEARNING STRATEGY

Remember

Listen selectively

Before you listen, look at the story. This helps you get ready to listen. Be ready to fill in the numbers you hear.

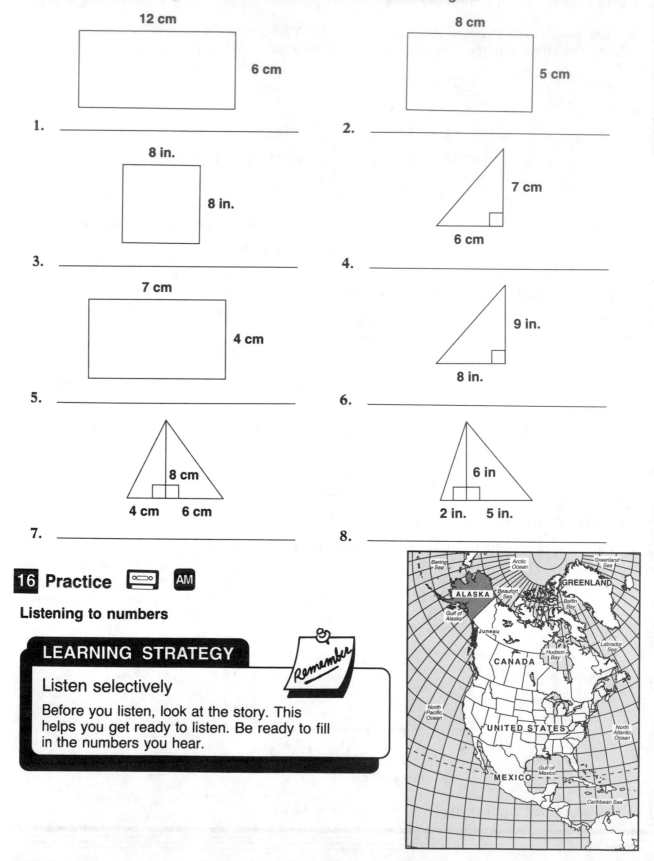

María, Jorge, and Lin had a class project in geography. They decided to report on Alaska. Listen to the ideas they report on Alaska. Fill in the numbers as you hear them.

The largest state in the United States is Alaska. The land area is _____ square miles. The next largest state, Texas, is less than _____ the size of Alaska. Alaska became the _____ state in the United States in _____ . The capital city is Juneau.

Alaska is in a far northwest part of North America and is connected on the south to Canada. Alaska has _____ major bodies of water surrounding it: the Pacific Ocean, the Bering Sea, and the Arctic Ocean. The land area has the tallest mountain in North America, Mt. McKinley. This huge mountain is _____ feet tall, or almost _____ meters.

Besides being the largest state, Alaska also has the fewest people. The population of Alaska in _____ was _____ . This was roughly a _____ increase over the _____ population. The population in 1980 included over _____ Native Americans, mostly Eskimos and Aleuts, and over _____ Asians.

17 | Extension

Averages and areas

1. Ask five classmates how many brothers they have and how many sisters they have. What is the average number of brothers and sisters among these five people?

    Average number of brothers: _____

    Average number of sisters: _____

2. Find the average length of the forearm for five boys and for five girls in your class. The forearm is measured from the tip of the elbow to the tip of the index finger.

    Average length for boys: _____

    Average length for girls: _____

3. Find the average number of hours five classmates do homework each week, watch TV each week, and work each week.

    Average hours homework: _____

    Average hours watch TV: _____

    Average hours work: _____

4. Look for some classroom objects that have the following shapes and find their area in square inches.

SHAPE	OBJECT	AREA
square	_____	_____
rectangle	_____	_____
triangle	_____	_____

UNIT 5: Learning Log

Check what you know. *Review* what you need to learn.

VOCABULARY

Operations and Related Words
— added to
— addend
— addition
— average
— divided by
— dividend
— division
— divisor
— equals
— equation
— factor
— multiplication
— number sentence
— product
— quotient
— subtraction
— sum
— times

Questions
— how many?
— how many more?
— how much?

Shapes
— equilateral triangle
— rectangle
— right triangle
— square
— triangle

Problem Solving Steps
— Understand the question
— Find the data
— Choose the operation
— Find the answer
— Check back

LEARNING STRATEGIES

I can:

— Use what I know to understand word problems.
— Make a picture or table to solve a problem.
— Cooperate with my classmates.
— Read selectively.
— Listen selectively.

CONTENT AND LANGUAGE

I can:

— Read about and understand multiplication and division.
— Write the words for a number sentence.
— Listen to and say number sentences.
— Read and use the Multiplication Table for the numbers 1–9.
— Find the average of five 2-digit numbers.
— Use the Problem Solving steps to solve word problems.
— Recognize geometric shapes: square, rectangle, right triangle, equilateral triangle.
— Find the area of these geometric shapes.
— Listen to and understand up to 6-digit numbers in the context of a paragraph.

SELF-CHECK QUESTIONS

What is interesting in Unit 5? _____

_____

_____

What is easy? _____

_____

_____

What is difficult? _____

_____

_____

How can you learn what is difficult? _____

_____

_____

Regions
of the World

UNIT
6

CONTENT KNOWLEDGE

Geographical regions of the
world: climate, natural
vegetation, animals

LEARNING STRATEGIES

Use what you know ▪ Make
inferences ▪ Take notes using
Idea Maps and T-lists ▪ Listen
selectively

LANGUAGE SKILLS

Present tense to describe
and to talk about facts ▪
Adjective + noun to describe

What do you know about geographical regions of the world?

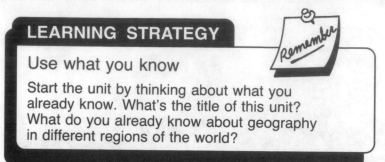

LEARNING STRATEGY

Use what you know

Start the unit by thinking about what you already know. What's the title of this unit? What do you already know about geography in different regions of the world?

A. **Look at the map. How many countries can you name? Write their names. Then write any information you know about each country's geography.**

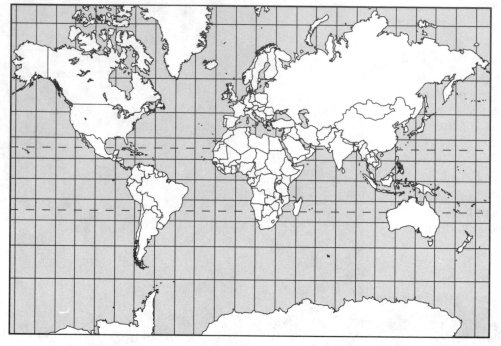

NAME OF COUNTRY

GEOGRAPHICAL INFORMATION

Brazil

hot weather, rainy, some jungles, some mountains

B. **Work with a classmate. Share information about the geography of different countries. Add new information to your lists in part A.**

C. Work with a classmate. Write the name of the geographical region under each picture. Use the words in the Word Box.

```
┌─────── WORD BOX ────────┐
   deciduous forest        mountain region
   desert                  northern forest
   grassland               polar region
   Mediterranean region    tropical rain forest
└─────────────────────────┘
```

1. _deciduous forest_

2. _____

3. _____

4. _____

5. _____

6. _____

7. _____

8. _____

D. Now answer these questions.

1. Which geographical region looks like your home country? _____

2. Which region looks like the place you live now? _____

3. Which region do you want to visit? _____

4. Why? _____

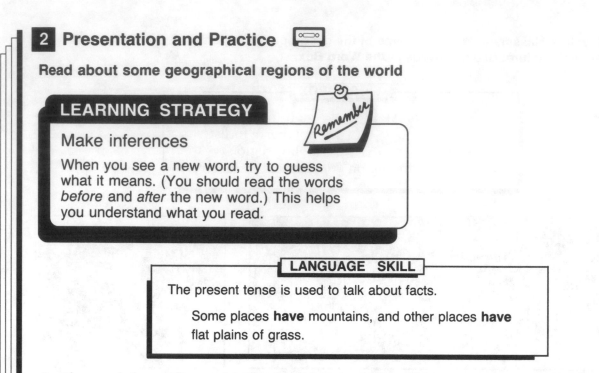

Read about some geographical regions of the world

LEARNING STRATEGY

Remember

Make inferences

When you see a new word, try to guess what it means. (You should read the words *before* and *after* the new word.) This helps you understand what you read.

LANGUAGE SKILL

The present tense is used to talk about facts.

Some places **have** mountains, and other places **have** flat plains of grass.

A. The earth has different kinds of land. Some places have mountains, and other places have flat plains of grass. Places can have different **climates** also. Some places are cold and have lots of snow. Other places are hot and have little rain.

We classify the world into eight different geographical **regions.** We look at location, climate, **vegetation** (or plants), and land forms (such as mountains) to classify geographical regions. For example, locations near the Equator usually have a hot and rainy climate, with beautiful tropical rain forests. However, mountains in these tropical areas can have a very cool climate and different kinds of vegetation. Each region has a different climate and different kinds of plants and animals. People in each region have different lives.

Choose the correct letter.

1. The climate of a region is
   a. its usual weather.
   b. its plants and animals.
   c. its land forms.

2. A region is a (an)
   a. kind of weather.
   b. area of land.
   c. kind of animal.

3. The vegetation in a region is
   a. its animals.
   b. its plants.
   c. its people.

B. Let's find out about the three forest regions. The *northern forest* has many pine trees that stay green all year. There isn't much rain, and the winters are very cold. Many animals have to **hibernate,** or sleep, through the winter. Other animals **migrate** to the south for the winter, because they need a warmer climate. There are northern forest regions in the north of Canada, Europe, and Asia.

Choose the correct letter.

4. When an animal hibernates,
   a. it lives in the forest.
   b. it hunts for food.
   c. it is not awake.

5. When an animal migrates,
   a. it lives in the forest.
   b. it travels to a different region.
   c. it hunts for food.

C. Trees in the **deciduous** *forest* grow new leaves in the spring. In the fall the leaves drop. The winters are cold, and the summers are hot. There is plenty of rain. The climate is pleasant, so lots of birds and animals live in this region. Many people also live in the deciduous forest regions of the world. These pleasant climate regions are mostly in Europe, Asia, and North America. There are many large cities in these areas.

Choose the correct letter.

6. In a deciduous forest, trees have leaves
   a. in summer.
   b. in winter.
   c. all year.

7. The climate in deciduous forest regions is
   a. hot all year.
   b. cold all year.
   c. both hot and cold.

D. In the *tropical rain forest* the trees and other vegetation stay green all year. The weather is very hot and wet all year long. The heavy rains make both big and little rivers. There are a lot of fish, birds, animals, and plants. There are some large cities, but many people live in small **villages.**

Choose the correct letter.

8. A tropical climate is
   a. rainy and quite warm.
   b. dry and cool.
   c. hot in the summer and cold in the winter.

9. A village is like a small
   a. town.
   b. forest.
   c. farm.

E. The three forest regions of the world have many trees. But the trees are different, because the land and the climate are different in each region. For example, northern forests have pine trees. Deciduous forests have trees with large leaves, and these leaves drop in the fall and grow again in the spring. In deciduous forest regions, the trees look dead in the winter. Tropical rain forests are very different, however. The trees are green all the time. There is no winter in tropical rain forest regions of the world.

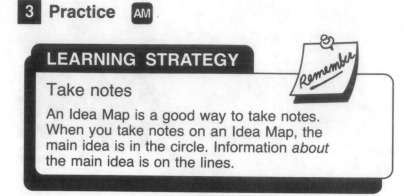

LEARNING STRATEGY

Remember

Take notes

An Idea Map is a good way to take notes.
When you take notes on an Idea Map, the
main idea is in the circle. Information *about*
the main idea is on the lines.

Reread 2 *Presentation*, pages 74–75. Then complete the Idea Maps below.
Write only the most important words.

Idea Maps about Forest Regions

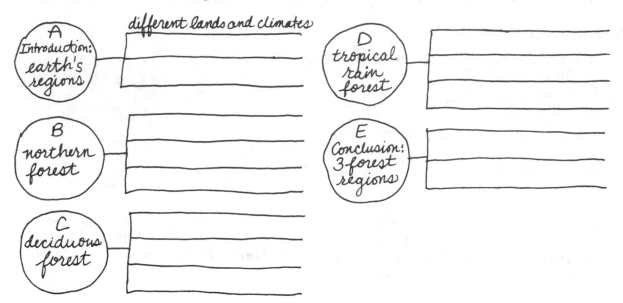

4 Practice

Go back to the reading passage on pages 74–75. List 10 adjectives and
the nouns they describe.

LANGUAGE SKILL
Use an *adjective* before a noun to describe something.
heavy rains   **big** rivers   **cold winters**

1. *cold winters*

2. _____

3. _____

4. _____

5. _____

6. _____

7. _____

8. _____

9. _____

10. _____

Presentation 🔲

Find out about three more geographical regions

REGION	TYPE OF CLIMATE	OTHER IDEAS
mountainous	cold air; rain and snowfall on one side of mountain; other side of mountain is dry; harsh winters	land is hard to live on; more plants at bottom of mountain; many trees; many minerals
Mediterranean	mild, rainy winters; hot, dry, sunny summers	many fish, plants, and animals; grass, trees; many people; a lot of farms (olives, citrus, grapes); land faces the sea
grassland	(a) *Savanna grasslands:* near Equator; hot all year; wet and dry seasons (b) *Prairie and steppe:* hot summer; cold winter; less rain than savannahs	grass is main plant; few trees; land is flat and low; many farms and ranches; many animals and people

6 **Practice** AM

Cross out the words or phrases in each column that do not belong. Use the information in the chart above.

LEARNING STRATEGY

Remember

Make inferences

Some words and phrases are not in the chart. You have to make *inferences*, or logical guesses. Remember to use what you already know about the world!

Mountainous	Grassland	Mediterranean
many trees	Africa	olive trees
~~warm~~	wet season	snow
snowy	hills	grass
long winter	many trees	many animals
flat	dry season	hard to live in
cold	grassy	near the ocean
many people	flat	Antarctica
strong animals	four seasons	wet summers
minerals	farms	lots of people
North America	hard to live in	no animals

7 Practice

Say whether each description is of a *mountainous, grassland,* or
Mediterranean region. Use the chart in *5 Presentation* and *what you
already know* to decide.

Mediterranean	1. In this region winters are not very cold.
_____	2. There aren't many trees in this region.
_____	3. This region has mountains.
_____	4. Here, there are many farms, but the winters are cold.
_____	5. This region probably exports minerals such as copper, gold, or silver.
_____	6. This region of the world exports fruit.
_____	7. People here live near the Equator.
_____	8. The climate in this region is very pleasant.
_____	9. Here, the climate in one town can be dry, and the climate of a town nearby can be wet.
_____	10. People here usually aren't very hot in the summer.

8 Preparation

Get ready to listen

A. Get ready to listen to information about two more regions of the
world: the polar and the desert regions. Work with a partner. Look at
the pictures on page 73 and use what you already know. What words
describe these two regions? List four words or ideas about these
climate regions.

DESERT

1. _____

2. _____

3. _____

4. _____

POLAR

1. _____

2. _____

3. _____

4. _____

B. Now talk with another pair of students. Add three more words or
ideas about polar and desert regions to your list.

DESERT

1. _____

2. _____

3. _____

POLAR

1. _____

2. _____

3. _____

Listen and take notes

A.   As you listen, use the T-list below to take notes.

> **LEARNING STRATEGY**
>
> Listen selectively and
> take notes
>
> T-lists are a good way to take notes and
> organize information. Remember to look at
> the T-list *before* you listen. Know what
> you're listening for.

1. Desert climate

   A. Days: _____very hot_____
   B. Nights: _____
   C. Rainfall: _____

2. Desert life

   A. Land: _____
   B. Plants and animals can live
      without much _____.
   C. People: _____
   D. People know how to _____
      _____ and _____.

3. Polar climate

   A. _____ of the desert.
   B. Very _____
   C. Summers: _____
      Winters: _____

4. Polar life

   A. Land: _____
   B. Plants: _____
   C. Not many _____.
   D. Animals have _____;
      people wear _____.

B.   Check your work with a partner.

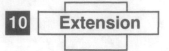

10 | Extension

Find out about different regions of the world

A. Interview a classmate. Write answers to the questions.

In your region of the world . . .

1. What clothes do people wear in January? _____
_____

2. What clothes do people wear in July? _____
_____

3. What sports can people play in the summer? _____
_____

4. Can people play different sports in the winter? Which ones? _____
_____

5. Which month is very wet? _____

6. Which month is very dry? _____

7. Do the leaves fall off the trees or do they stay green all year? _____

8. What are some exports (fruit? coffee? minerals?) of your region? _____
_____

9. Classify the place you are from into one of the eight regions of the world. _____
_____

B. Now share the information you learned about your classmate with the class. Begin as follows:

_____ is from _____.
(classmate's name)   (city/town, country)

UNIT 6: Learning Log

Check what you know. *Review* what you need to learn.

VOCABULARY

Geographical Regions
— deciduous forest
— desert
— grassland
— Mediterranean
— mountainous
— northern forest
— polar
— tropical rain forest

Geography Nouns
— animal
— city
— climate
— Equator
— fall
— farm
— grass
— land
— location
— mineral
— mountain
— pine trees
— plain
— plant
— prairie
— ranch
— region
— river
— savanna
— spring
— steppe
— summer
— town
— vegetation
— village
— winter

Adjectives
— cold
— cool
— dead
— different
— dry
— flat
— geographical
— grassy
— green
— harsh
— heavy
— hot
— large
— low
— mild
— pleasant
— rainy
— small
— snowy
— tropical
— warm
— wet

Verbs
— export
— hibernate
— migrate

LEARNING STRATEGIES

I can:
— Use what I know to understand new information.
— Make inferences to guess at meanings of new words.
— Take notes using Idea Maps.
— Listen selectively and take notes using a T-list.

CONTENT AND LANGUAGE

I can:
— Identify the geographical regions of the world.
— Read and answer questions about three different forest regions, then make Idea Maps about the forest regions.
— Use adjectives to describe nouns.
— Read about and identify characteristics of mountainous, Mediterranean, and grassland regions.
— Listen and take notes on information about desert and polar regions.
— Interview a classmate about life in one geographical region.

SELF-CHECK QUESTIONS

What is interesting in Unit 6?

_____

_____

What is easy?

_____

_____

What is difficult?

_____

_____

How can you learn what is difficult?

_____

_____

Living Things

CONTENT KNOWLEDGE

Cells and growth ▪ Characteristics of living things ▪ Some differences between plants and animals

LEARNING STRATEGIES

Use what you know ▪ Take notes using an Idea Map and a diagram ▪ Listen selectively ▪ Cooperate

LANGUAGE SKILLS

Present tense to describe and to talk about facts ▪ Past tense to talk about past events

1 Preparation

What do you know about living things?

Living and Nonliving Things

1. Which of the things in the drawing above are alive?

    baby
    _____ _____ _____
    _____ _____ _____
    _____ _____ _____
    _____ _____ _____
    _____ _____ _____

2. Name five other things that are alive.

    _____ _____ _____
         _____ _____

3. Name five things in the drawing that are *not* alive (nonliving).

    _____ _____ _____
         _____ _____

2 Presentation

Read about cells

All living things have five characteristics. The first characteristic is: **They are made of cells.** Cells are very small and very active. Your body has millions of cells. But some living things have only one cell.

Because cells are so small, you need a microscope to see a cell. Cells are very important, because all living things are made of cells. You are going to learn more about cells later in this unit.

Microscopes help you see very small things.

3 Practice AM

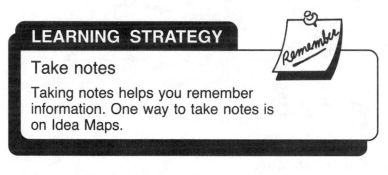

LEARNING STRATEGY

Take notes

Taking notes helps you remember information. One way to take notes is on Idea Maps.

Put information from the reading passage above onto the first Idea Map below. (You can't finish the Idea Map called "Living Things" yet. You need information from other parts of this unit. Right now, you should only complete the Idea Map called "Cells.")

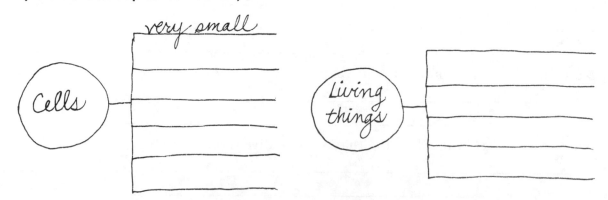

very small

Cells

Living things

More about living things

You know about one characteristic of living things: They are made of cells. Look at some other characteristics of living things.

1.   **They are made of cells.**

2.   **They take in matter, because they need energy.**

3.   **They reproduce.**

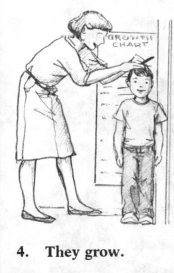

4.   **They grow.**

5.   **They react to change.**

5 **Practice**

Add the information above to the Idea Map called "Living Things" on page 84.

┌─────── LANGUAGE SKILL ───────┐

Use the present tense to talk about scientific facts.

Cells **are** very small.
Animals and plants **reproduce.**

6 Presentation

Read about "taking in matter"

What does it mean to "take in matter?" Well, what did you eat for dinner last night? When you ate dinner, you took in matter. We take in matter, because we need energy—energy to move, energy to talk, energy to live. Is "eating" the same thing as "taking in matter?" The answer is: sometimes.

Animals eat. That's taking in matter. They use the food (or matter) to get energy. Not all living things eat food to get energy. Plants, for example, don't eat food, but they do take in matter. How? They take in matter such as water and minerals with their roots, and they take in sunlight and air with their leaves. They use the water, minerals, air, and sunlight to make food. And the food gives them energy! So, we can say that plants make their own energy.

Plants and animals are different. But they both take in matter, because they both need energy.

LEARNING STRATEGY

Take notes

Sometimes you can take good notes with a *diagram.* A diagram makes a strong picture in your mind.

Take notes on the reading passage about "taking in matter" using the diagram below. Complete the diagram with words and phrases from the Word Box.

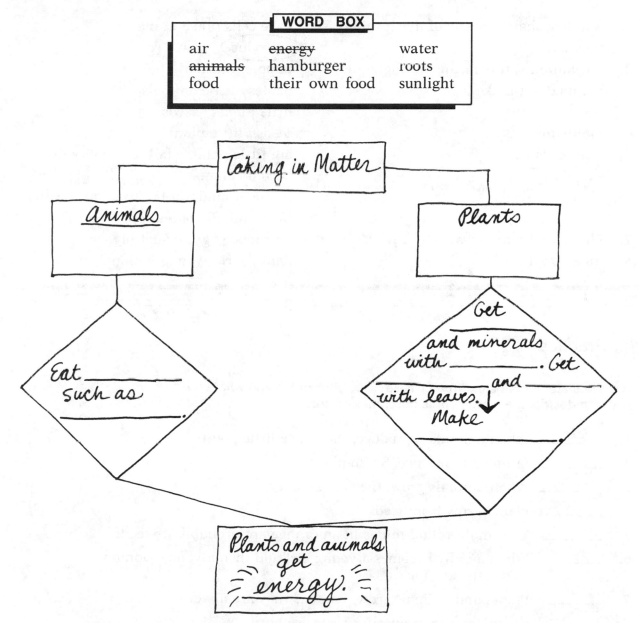

WORD BOX

air	~~energy~~	water
~~animals~~	hamburger	roots
food	their own food	sunlight

Taking in Matter

Animals

Plants

Eat _____ such as _____.

Get _____ and minerals with _____. Get _____ and _____ with leaves. Make _____.

Plants and animals get energy.

Find out about "reproducing" and "growing"

LEARNING STRATEGY

Remember

Listen selectively

What two places should you look *before* you listen? (HINT: One is the title!) Why? Where else should you look?

Listen. Take notes below and circle the words you hear. There may be more than one answer.

1. Another characteristic of living things is they . . .

   have cells / take in matter / (reproduce) / grow / react

2. For animals, this means having . . .

   puppies / kittens / babies

3. Plants don't make . . .

   babies / little animals / little plants / seeds

4. Plants make . . .

   seeds / little plants / dirt

5. The seeds . . .

   are little plants / fall to the ground / become plants

6. There are seeds . . .

   in the ground / in the tree / in the air / in the middle of an apple

7. Plants and animals also . . .

   reproduce / grow / get bigger

8. An example is a . . .

   baby / girl / woman / plant

9 Practice AM

Are the statements below true or false? Use your notes and *what you know* to decide. If a statement is false, make it true.

1. __false__ When animals reproduce, they have little ~~plants~~. *animals*

2. _____ Animals reproduce. So do plants.

3. _____ When animals grow, they get smaller.

4. _____ Plants grow from seeds.

5. _____ The small, round things in an orange are probably its seeds.

6. _____ When a baby becomes a young girl and then a young woman, she's reproducing.

7. _____ Plants and animals grow, because they are alive.

8. _____ When a cat reproduces, kittens are born.

9. _____ When an animal reproduces, seeds fall to the ground.

10 Presentation 📼

What about "reacting to change?"

We've already learned that living things are made of cells and that they take in matter. We also know that living things reproduce and grow. What is another characteristic of living things?

Well, living things react to change. What does that mean? Here's an example: It's cool in the morning, so you wear a sweater. The temperature goes up (the *change*). You take your sweater off (you *react*). Here are some other examples:

11 Practice 🅰🅼

Identify changes and reactions

A. In the sentences below, underline the change. Circle the reaction.

1. The deer is eating. A mountain lion appears. The deer runs.
2. It's winter. The tree has no leaves. Spring comes. Small leaves grow on the tree.
3. A cat is sleeping in the sun. A dog comes into the yard. The cat wakes up and climbs a tree.
4. You're watching television. Your little sister changes the program. You yell.
5. It's a beautiful day. People are eating outside. Suddenly, it starts raining. Everyone goes inside.
6. You're crossing the street. A car suddenly appears, and you're in its path. You jump out of the way and scream at the driver.

B. Now write three *change-reaction* scenes of your own.

1. _____

2. _____

3. _____

C. *Think.* Can the reaction come before the change? Why or why not?

D. What other *reactions* could there be? Work with a partner. Discuss a new reaction for each change. Write the new reaction.

1. A cat is sleeping in the sun. A dog comes into the yard.

_____

2. You're watching television. Your little sister changes the program.

_____

3. You're crossing the street. A car suddenly appears, and you're in its path.

_____

12 Practice

Look back at the five characteristics of living things listed in *4 Presentation*, page 85. Read the 12 activities below. Identify each as characteristic 1, 2, 3, 4, or 5.

____ **1.** A dog eats a bone.

____ **2.** A bird sees a cat. The bird flies to a tree.

____ **3.** A cat has six kittens.

____ **4.** It's cold. You put on a sweater.

____ **5.** Your shoes are getting too small.

____ **6.** Because your shoes are too small, you buy a new pair.

____ **7.** You look at a leaf under a microscope.
You see this:

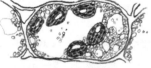

____ **8.** A big fish eats a small fish.

____ **9.** A chicken lays an egg and sits on it.

____ **10.** The little boy can reach the light switch today.

____ **11.** You look at a piece of skin under a microscope.
You see this:

____ **12.** It gets dark. The owl wakes up.

13 Presentation 📼

Read about "cells" and "growth"

You were once a small baby. Now you're big. How did your body grow? The answer is: Your cells grew, and your body got more cells. So you got bigger!

Let's look at how one cell grows. The cell gets energy from food. It grows bigger. When it gets to a certain size, the cell divides, or **splits.** This means that one cell becomes two cells.

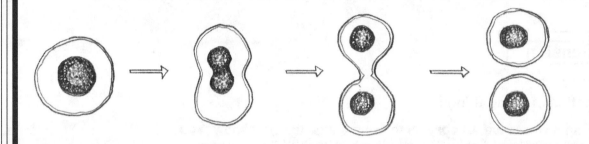

The two new cells are alike. These cells grow. Then each cell splits. So, from that first cell, now there are four cells. And that's how living things grow!

14 Practice

Solve this math and science problem. An animal starts with one cell. This first cell divides in two minutes. How many cells are there after six minutes? To help you solve the problem, draw the cells as they divide.

START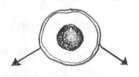

2 minutes

4 minutes

6 minutes

15 Practice

A. *Do not* look back in this unit. From memory, name five characteristics of living things.

1. _____
2. _____
3. _____
4. _____
5. _____

B. Check your answers with a partner. Did you each name at least four characteristics?

16 Extension

Characteristics of living things

A. Work with a classmate. Choose three living things that you know. You can choose plants and animals (including humans). Write a paragraph about each living thing. In the paragraph, describe the living thing. Be sure to describe the characteristics that make it a living thing.

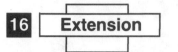

LEARNING STRATEGY

Remember

Cooperate

When you work with a classmate you can get more ideas. This helps you learn.

LANGUAGE SKILL

Use the *past tense* to talk about *past events*.

I **planted** some seeds and **watered** them. In six weeks the seeds **grew** and I **had** beautiful plants. I **forgot** to water my plants for a week. Some of the plants **died**.

BUT: Use the *present tense* to talk about *science facts*.

Each plant **has** many cells. Each cell **is** very small.

---

1. Name of Living Thing _____

_____

_____

_____

_____

_____

2. Name of Living Thing _____

_____

_____

_____

_____

3. Name of Living Thing _____

_____

_____

_____

_____

B. Now work with two other classmates. Don't tell them the name of your living things. Read your paragraphs to your classmates. Can they guess your living things?

C. Ask your classmates to read your paragraphs and to circle the words that tell about the characteristics of living things.

UNIT 7: Learning Log

Check what you know. *Review* what you need to learn.

VOCABULARY

Science Nouns
— air
— cell
— change
— characteristic
— energy
— matter
— microscope
— mineral
— reaction
— sunlight

Adjectives
— alive
— living
— nonliving

Parts of Plants
— leaf (leaves)
— root
— seed

Useful Verbs
— divide
— grow
— react
— reproduce
— split
— take in

LEARNING STRATEGIES

I can:

— Use what I know to understand new information.
— Take notes using an Idea Map.
— Take notes using a diagram.
— Listen selectively.
— Cooperate with classmates.

CONTENT AND LANGUAGE

I can:

— Identify living and nonliving things.
— Read and take notes about the characteristics of living things.
— Listen to information about reproducing and growing.
— Read how living things respond to change, and identify changes and reactions.
— Identify the characteristics of living things.
— Read about cells and growth, and solve a math problem about cells.
— Evaluate my own learning.
— Write about living things that I know.

SELF-CHECK QUESTIONS

What is interesting in Unit 7?

_____

_____

What is easy?

_____

_____

What is difficult?

_____

_____

How can you learn what is difficult?

_____

_____

Living in the
United States

UNIT 8

CONTENT KNOWLEDGE

Personal rights and responsibilities ▪ Laws ▪ Democracy as a form of government ▪ Societal rights and responsibilities

LEARNING STRATEGIES

Use what you know ▪ Make inferences ▪ Listen selectively ▪ Take notes ▪ Read selectively ▪ Cooperate

LANGUAGE SKILLS

Should + verb ▪ *Can* + verb ▪ *Have/has to* + verb ▪ Using *because* to give reasons

1 Preparation

Family rules

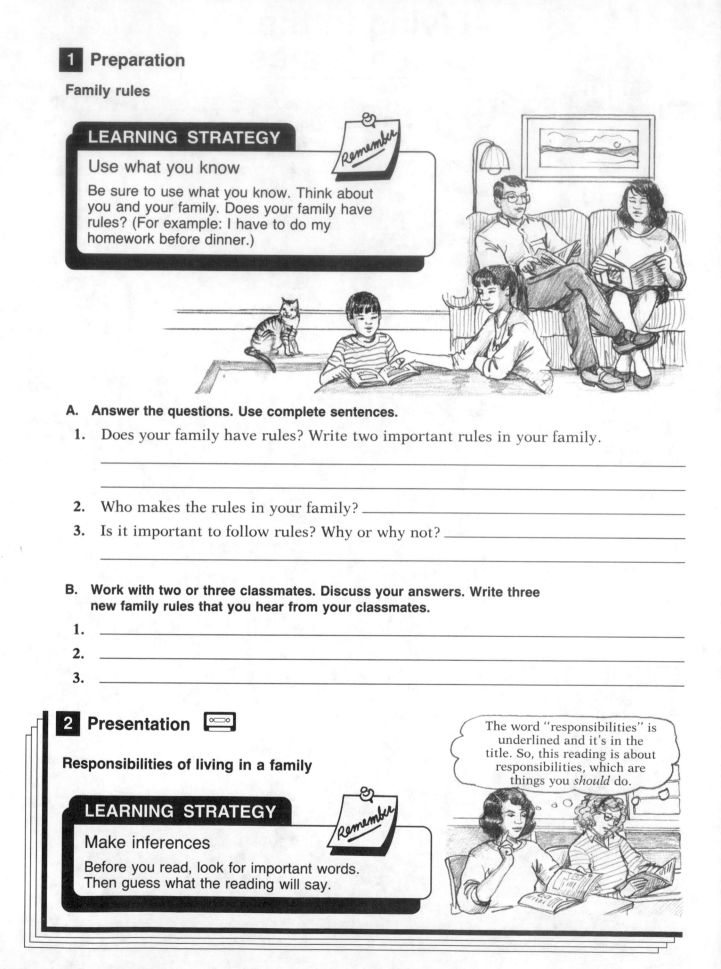

> ### LEARNING STRATEGY
>
> **Use what you know**
>
> Be sure to use what you know. Think about you and your family. Does your family have rules? (For example: I have to do my homework before dinner.)

A. Answer the questions. Use complete sentences.

1. Does your family have rules? Write two important rules in your family.

   _____

   _____

2. Who makes the rules in your family? _____

3. Is it important to follow rules? Why or why not? _____

   _____

B. Work with two or three classmates. Discuss your answers. Write three new family rules that you hear from your classmates.

1. _____

2. _____

3. _____

2 Presentation

Responsibilities of living in a family

> ### LEARNING STRATEGY
>
> **Make inferences**
>
> Before you read, look for important words. Then guess what the reading will say.

> The word "responsibilities" is underlined and it's in the title. So, this reading is about responsibilities, which are things you *should* do.

Isabel Rodríguez and her family

My name is Isabel Rodríguez. I live with my family. In my family, I have three <u>responsibilities</u>. First, I should be a good student. This means I should listen in class, read my books, and do my homework on time. Second, I should help my family. I help clean the house, and sometimes I mow the lawn. And third, I should help my younger brother and sister. Sometimes I watch them for my parents, and sometimes I help them with their homework. All of these jobs are my responsibilities. These are the jobs that I *should* do.

Isabel   Elena   Anita   Manuel   Carlos

3 Practice

Complete the following table. Work with a partner.

ISABEL'S RESPONSIBILITIES AT HOME	MY RESPONSIBILITIES AT HOME	MY PARTNER'S RESPONSIBILITIES AT HOME
1. *be a good student*	1.	1.
2.	2.	2.
3.	3.	3.

4 Practice

What responsibilities do other people have? Work with a partner. Write complete sentences using *should* + verb.

LANGUAGE SKILL

Use **should** + *verb* to talk about responsibilities.

I **should do** my homework.
My sister **should do** the dishes on Tuesdays.

---

1. **Teachers:** a. *Teachers should explain clearly.*

                  b.

                  c.

2. **Parents:** a.

                  b.

                  c.

3. **Friends:** a.

                  b.

                  c.

5 Presentation

Listen to information about rights

> **LEARNING STRATEGY**
>
> *Remember*
>
> **Listen selectively and take notes**
>
> Before you listen, look at the questions. This
> helps you know what information you need.
> Then take notes as you listen.

1. Who is speaking? _____

2. The speaker has responsibilities and _____ .

3. What is a right? _____

4. The speaker tells you about some of her rights. Name two. _____
   _____

5. Why does the speaker have these rights? _____

6 Practice

**Write three rights you have in your school and in your community. Then
talk to a classmate. What rights does he or she have?**

MY RIGHTS

1. _____
2. _____
3. _____

MY PARTNER'S RIGHTS

1. _____
2. _____
3. _____

7 Practice

**What rights do other people have? Work with a small group. Write
complete sentences using *can* + verb.**

> **LANGUAGE SKILL**
>
> Use **can** + *verb* to talk about rights.
>
> Isabel **can choose** some of her classes.
> I **can choose** to go to the movies on Saturday.

1. Teachers: a. *Teachers can choose when to give homework.*

              b. _____

              c. _____

2. Parents: a. _____

b. _____

c. _____

3. Friends: a. _____

b. _____

c. _____

8 Practice AM

A. Mark with an "X" which activities are rights, which activities are responsibilities, and which are both.

THINGS I DO	RIGHT	RESPONSIBILITY	BOTH
1. Pay for food in a store.	_____	*X*	_____
2. Put my lunch bag in the trash when I'm done.	_____	_____	_____
3. Make money when I work.	_____	_____	_____
4. Go to school.	_____	_____	_____
5. Listen to my parents.	_____	_____	_____
6. Use the library.	_____	_____	_____
7. Do my homework.	_____	_____	_____
8. Eat in the cafeteria.	_____	_____	_____
9. Participate in class.	_____	_____	_____
10. Return my library books.	_____	_____	_____

B. Compare your answers with a partner. Do you agree? Discuss your answers.

9 Presentation

Read about laws

The United States is a large country with many people.
Americans go to work, buy things, drive cars, and see their friends.
These are their rights. They can do these things without problems
because of **laws.** Laws are like classroom rules—they help people
live and work together.

Laws are things you *have to* do. For example, you have to drive
on the right side of the street in this country because of a law. Laws
also protect people. For example, because it's the law, you have to
drive slowly near a school. Laws also tell what you *cannot* do. For
example, you cannot steal food from a store, and you cannot throw
rocks at cars. Everybody has to obey the laws.

10 Practice AM

**Work in a group of three or five students. Read each law below. Do you
think the law is *good* or *bad*? Vote in your group. The majority wins! If
you think the law is bad, how would you change it?**

		GOOD	BAD
1.	You cannot drive more than 55 miles per hour.	____	____
2.	You have to stop for a school bus when its lights are flashing.	____	____
3.	You have to go to school until you are 16.	____	____
4.	You have to pay tax money to the government.	____	____
5.	You cannot smoke on most airplanes.	____	____
6.	You have to stop your car for a red traffic light.	____	____
7.	You cannot ride the subway for free.	____	____
8.	You cannot enter the U.S. without a visa.	____	____
9.	In some states, you have to wear a seatbelt in the car.	____	____
10.	You cannot drive a car without a license.	____	____

11 Practice

Write three laws that you know. Use complete sentences with *have to* or *has to* + verb.

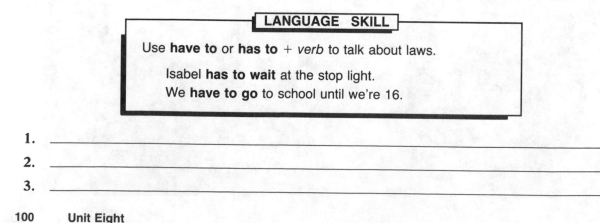

```
┌─────────── LANGUAGE  SKILL ───────────┐
  Use have to or has to + verb to talk about laws.

  Isabel has to wait at the stop light.
  We have to go to school until we're 16.
└────────────────────────────────────────┘
```

1. _____

2. _____

3. _____

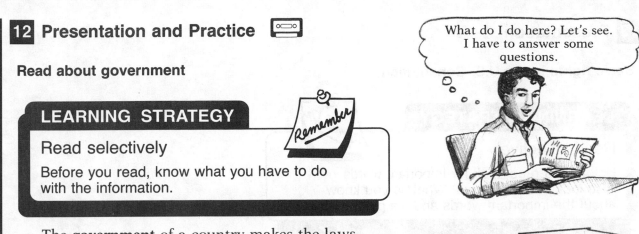

Read about government

LEARNING STRATEGY

Remember

Read selectively

Before you read, know what you have to do
with the information.

The **government** of a country makes the laws.
There are many forms of government. A
democracy is one form. In a democracy people
have many rights. For example, they can choose
their leaders. They vote for the person they like
best. The person with the most votes wins, or is
elected. This person **represents** the people's ideas
in the government.

The people in government represent the ideas and opinions of
the citizens. For this reason, the government in the United States is
called a **representative democracy.** In the U.S. a **citizen** is someone
who can vote and who has other basic rights.

A.   Answer the questions below. Use complete sentences.

1.   What is one type of government?

_____

2.   Can you think of other types of government? _____

_____

3.   In a democracy, what is one example of a citizen's rights?

_____

4.   When a person is elected in a representative democracy, which of the
following are true?

   a.   The person is in government forever.
   b.   The person got more votes than anyone else.
   c.   The person represents other people's ideas and opinions in the government.
   d.   Citizens voted for the person.

B.   Check your work with a partner. Discuss any differences.

LEARNING STRATEGY

Remember

Cooperate

Working together helps you learn.

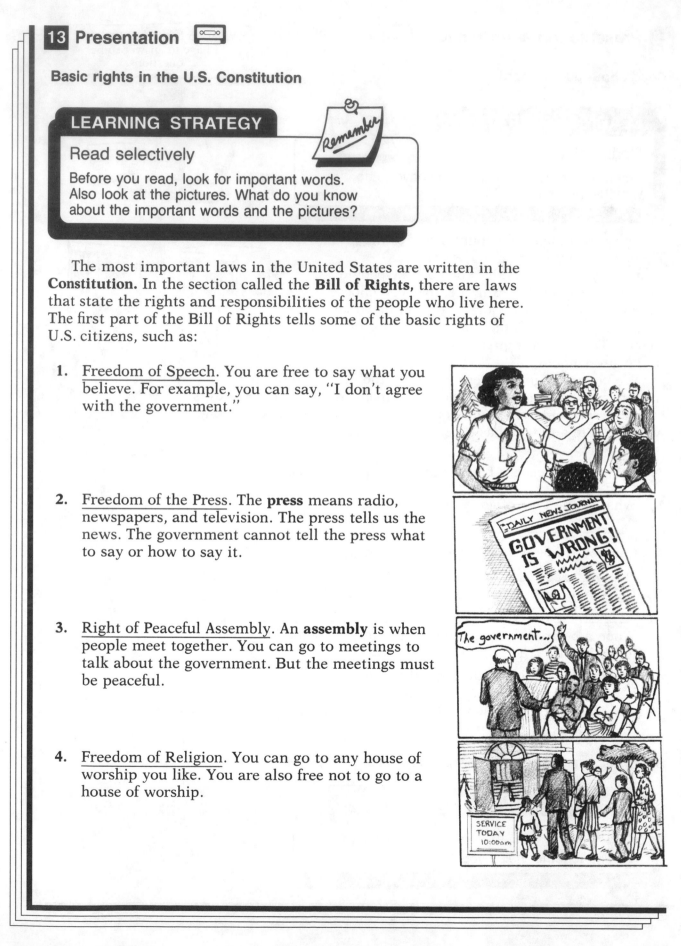
Basic rights in the U.S. Constitution

> **LEARNING STRATEGY**
>
> *Remember*
>
> **Read selectively**
>
> Before you read, look for important words.
> Also look at the pictures. What do you know
> about the important words and the pictures?

The most important laws in the United States are written in the
Constitution. In the section called the **Bill of Rights,** there are laws
that state the rights and responsibilities of the people who live here.
The first part of the Bill of Rights tells some of the basic rights of
U.S. citizens, such as:

1. <u>Freedom of Speech</u>. You are free to say what you
   believe. For example, you can say, "I don't agree
   with the government."

2. <u>Freedom of the Press</u>. The **press** means radio,
   newspapers, and television. The press tells us the
   news. The government cannot tell the press what
   to say or how to say it.

3. <u>Right of Peaceful Assembly</u>. An **assembly** is when
   people meet together. You can go to meetings to
   talk about the government. But the meetings must
   be peaceful.

4. <u>Freedom of Religion</u>. You can go to any house of
   worship you like. You are also free not to go to a
   house of worship.

14 Practice

A. There are 10 activities listed below. For each one, write the freedom it represents: Freedom of Religion, Freedom of Speech, Freedom of the Press, or Right of Peaceful Assembly. If the activity represents *none* of these rights, write "none."

_____F of Speech_____ 1. You think a leader is dishonest. You write an angry letter to him.

_____ 2. The newspaper writes a funny article about the president of the U.S.

_____ 3. The president of the U.S. lets angry people meet outside his home.

_____ 4. You go to a Catholic church, and your best friend goes to a Jewish synagogue.

_____ 5. Students get together to eat lunch.

_____ 6. Leaders don't agree with the president, and they say so.

_____ 7. You state your beliefs and get elected to the government.

_____ 8. Mrs. Spencer never goes to church.

_____ 9. Citizens are standing outside City Hall. They have signs saying, "The mayor is wrong!"

_____ 10. Experts talk on the radio. They say negative things about politicians.

B. Compare your answers with a partner. Do you agree? Discuss.

15 Presentation and Practice

Limits to freedom

Listen to the passage. Complete the sentences as you listen. Then answer the questions that have been asked. Also tell why.

> **┤ LANGUAGE SKILL ├**
>
> Use **because** to give reasons in your answer.
>
> You should not yell "Fire!" when there is no fire **because** people might be hurt.

1. You yell _____ and there is no _____ . Is this
   freedom of _____ ?
   Answer: _____
   Why? _____

2. People _____ drugs near your house. Is this freedom of

_____ ?

Answer: _____

Why? _____

3. The _____ says that you _____ some money.

But you _____ . Is this freedom of _____ ?

Answer: _____

Why? _____

16 Presentation 🔲

Responsibilities in the United States

> **LEARNING STRATEGY**
>
> **Read selectively**
>
> Look at the title and the underlined words to help you know what the topic is. Then look at the T-list in *17 Practice*, page 105. What do you need to find in the reading?

People who live in a democracy have **responsibilities.** Some of these responsibilities are required by laws. These are things that people *have to* do:

1. <u>Obey the laws</u>. People have to obey the laws of the government. For example, you have to obey the laws for driving cars. You cannot hurt other people or steal.
2. <u>Pay taxes</u>. You have to pay money to the government. This money is called **taxes.** Taxes pay for roads, schools, police, firefighters, and other things that people need.
3. <u>Serve in the military</u>. The military is the army, navy, and air force. The military defends the country. Citizens have to serve in the military if the government asks them to.

People have other responsibilities that are not required by law. These are things that people *should* do:

1. <u>Vote</u>. People in a democracy have a responsibility to vote. They vote for the leaders in the government.
2. <u>Be informed</u>. People have a responsibility to be informed. They should know about problems in their country.
3. <u>Take action</u>. People should also take action to *solve* problems in the community. People should have meetings and work together in groups. Some examples of problems in the community are dangerous roads and schools that need more money. When necessary, people should ask the government for help.

17 Practice AM

Use the T-list below to take notes on the reading in *16 Presentation*.

Responsibilities in the United States

Responsibilities required by law	Definition: <u>Things people have to do</u> Examples: 1. _____ 2. _____ 3. _____
Responsibilities not required by law	Definition: _____ Examples: 1. _____ 2. _____ 3. _____

18 Extension

What do you think?

1. Interview two people in your community. Ask them this question: What are the most important responsibilities for citizens?

   Person 1: _____

   _____

   Person 2: _____

   _____

2. Which one responsibility do *you* think is the most important? Give a reason, using **because**.

   _____

   _____

3. Which two rights do *you* think are the most important for citizens to have? Use **because** in the answer.

   _____

   _____

   _____

Now, share your answers with a small group. Were your answers the same as or different from your classmates'?

UNIT 8: Learning Log

Check what you know. *Review* what you need to learn.

VOCABULARY

General Terms
— Bill of Rights
— citizen
— Constitution
— elected
— freedom
— law
— limits
— military
— obey
— represent
— responsibility
— right
— rule
— taxes

Types of Government
— democracy
— representative democracy

Responsibilities
— be informed
— obey the law
— pay taxes
— serve in the military
— vote

Basic Rights
— freedom of peaceful assembly
— freedom of press
— freedom of religion
— freedom of speech

LEARNING STRATEGIES

I can:
— Use what I know to understand new information.
— Make inferences to understand new words.
— Listen selectively and take notes.
— Read selectively and take notes using a T-list.
— Cooperate with my classmates.

CONTENT AND LANGUAGE

I can:
— Understand what rules are and give examples.
— Read about and understand responsibilities.
— Use **should** + *verb* to give examples of responsibilities.
— Listen to and understand information about rights.
— Use **can** + *verb* to give examples of rights.
— Recognize rights and responsibilities from examples given.
— Read and understand about laws.
— Use **have to** and **has to** + *verb* to write about laws.
— Read about and take notes on government.
— Read about basic rights in the U.S. Constitution.
— Recognize examples of freedom of speech, the press, peaceful assembly, and religion.
— Use **because** to give reasons why examples given are not basic freedoms.
— Use a T-list to take notes on responsibilities.

SELF-CHECK QUESTIONS

What is interesting in Unit 8?

_____

_____

What is easy?

_____

_____

What is difficult?

_____

_____

How can you learn what is difficult?

_____

_____

The Beginning of History

CONTENT KNOWLEDGE

Timelines • B.C. and A.D. •
First Americans • Early
civilizations • Map skills

LEARNING STRATEGIES

Use what you know • Make a
timeline • Read selectively •
Make inferences • Classify •
Cooperate

LANGUAGE SKILLS

Past tense statements • Simple
present to state facts

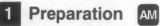

1 Preparation AM

What do you know about history?

> **LEARNING STRATEGY** *Remember*
>
> **Use what you know**
>
> What's the name of this unit? What do you already know about history? Do you know the name of a famous person in history? Do you know about an important event in history?

A. History is the story of the past. You know about the history of your own life. The first *event* of your life is written on the chart below. Write the first *date* in your life story (for example, 1/25/79). Then write other important events and dates in your life.

┌─────────────────── **LANGUAGE SKILL** ───────────────────┐

Use the past tense to talk about events in the past.

VERB	PAST FORM	VERB	PAST FORM
be: is	was	learn	learned
be: are	were	make	made
come	came	meet	met
do	did	see	saw
go	went	talk	talked
happen	happened	travel	traveled
have	had	write	wrote

My Life History

DATE	EVENT
	I was born.

B. Make a timeline of your life. Then talk to a classmate and make a timeline of your classmate's life. Use this timeline as a model.

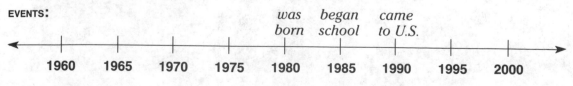

EVENTS:

was born   began school   came to U.S.

←———1960———1965———1970———1975———1980———1985———1990———1995———2000———→

Make a timeline

A timeline shows the *sequence* of events. It is a chart of what happened first, second, third, etc. Timelines help you understand history.

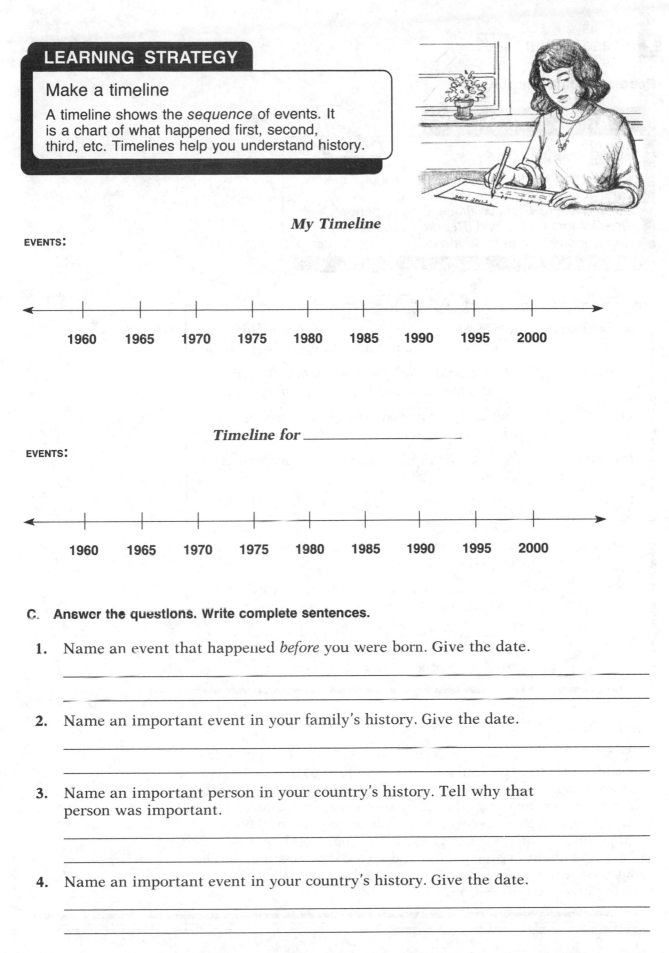

My Timeline

EVENTS:

◄————┼———————┼———————┼———————┼———————┼———————┼———————┼———————┼———————┼————►
    1960   1965   1970   1975   1980   1985   1990   1995   2000

Timeline for _____

EVENTS:

◄————┼———————┼———————┼———————┼———————┼———————┼———————┼———————┼———————┼————►
    1960   1965   1970   1975   1980   1985   1990   1995   2000

C. Answer the questions. Write complete sentences.

1. Name an event that happened *before* you were born. Give the date.

    _____

    _____

2. Name an important event in your family's history. Give the date.

    _____

    _____

3. Name an important person in your country's history. Tell why that person was important.

    _____

    _____

4. Name an important event in your country's history. Give the date.

    _____

    _____

Read and think about history

LEARNING STRATEGY

Read selectively

Remember, before you read, think about what you have to learn. Look at the questions in *3 Practice* first—then you know what information to find. *Reading selectively* helps you read and understand.

Remember

WORD BOX

archeologist:	A scientist who studies prehistoric or historic people by examining the things they made.
artifact:	Any object made by man; refers especially to objects made thousands of years ago.
buried:	Any thing or person put into the ground and covered with earth.
invent:	To make or produce something for the first time.
invention:	Something that is new and made for the first time.
painting:	A picture or drawing made with paints (colors).
ruins:	What is left of an old building or city many years later.
sculpture:	An art form (such as a statue) that shows people, animals, etc. made in stone, marble, bronze, or other material.

What is history?

History is the story of people in different times. History tells us about important people and events. It also tells us about the lives of ordinary people long ago. We know about history, because we can still see some of the things that early people made, such as paintings and sculpture. We can even see the ruins of very old buildings.

Most importantly, we can read the writing of early people. Early writing was about events, people, and ideas. We know a great deal about these early people, because they could write. History starts with the invention of writing.

**Hieroglyphics
(Egypt)**

**Cuneiform
(Middle East)**

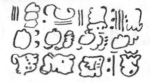

**Maya Hieroglyphs
(Central America)**

The period before the invention of writing is called **prehistory.**
Prehistory means "before history." Archeologists are scientists who
study prehistory. They study artifacts, or things prehistoric people
made, and find out many things about their lives. The artifacts are
usually buried in the ground in a place where people used to live.
Because of the work of archeologists, we know a lot about
prehistoric people. But we do not know their names or personal
ideas—they did not know how to write.

3 Practice

A.   Look at the pictures. Which ones are artifacts? Write the letters. _____

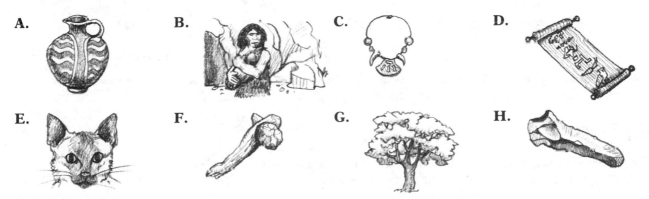

A.

B.

C.

D.

E.

F.

G.

H.

B.   Now answer these questions. Write complete sentences.

> ┤ **LANGUAGE SKILL** ├
>
> Use the simple present to talk about things we know.
>
> History **tells** about events long ago.
> Archeologists **study** prehistoric man.

1.   What is history? _____

_____

2.   How do we know about history? _____

_____

3.   How do we know about prehistory? _____

_____

4 Presentation 📼

Counting time

Time can be counted in different ways. Many people count time in years (1 year = 365 days) and in centuries (1 century = 100 years). Some people think of the year that Jesus Christ was born as the year 0. Events *after* the year 0 are A.D. *(Anno Domini*, Latin for *In the Year of Our Lord)*. We are living in A.D. What year A.D. are we living in? Events *before* the year 0 are B.C. *(Before Christ)*. Study the timeline below.

LEARNING STRATEGY

Remember

Use a timeline

Timelines show *sequence.* They tell you if one event came before or after another event. Timelines help you understand history.

NOW

| 6000 | 5000 | 4000 | 3000 | 2000 | 1000 | 0 | 1000 | 2000 |

◄────────── Years B.C. ──────────┼────── Years A.D. ──────►

---

5 Practice

Work with a partner. Use the timeline above to solve the problems. For #3–7, write the events mentioned on the timeline.

1. There were _____ years between 5000 B.C. and 1500 B.C.
2. A person was born in 45 B.C. How old was that person in 10 A.D.? _____
3. The Bronze Age (when people made tools from bronze) went on for about 2000 years. It started about 3000 B.C. The Bronze Age ended about _____ B.C.
4. The first city in the world was probably Jericho, found in what is today the Middle East. It was built about 8000 B.C. The first pyramids in Egypt were built in about 2800 B.C. There were about _____ years between Jericho and the pyramids.

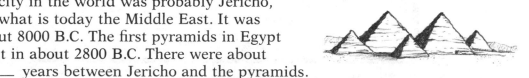

5. People in Sumer, an early city in the Middle East, invented the wheel in about 3500 B.C. People in Egypt invented the 365-day calendar in about 3000 B.C. Which was first, the wheel or the calendar? _____
6. People in Mexico were growing corn in about 5000 B.C. About how many years ago was that? _____
7. One of the first cities in America was Teotihuacan in Mexico. It began to be important in about 300 B.C. and was destroyed in about 900 A.D. For how long was this ancient city important? _____

6 Presentation

The first Americans

Thousands of years ago, America did not have any people. America had only forests, rivers, lakes, animals, and plants. The first people came to America 25,000 or more years ago. We call the first Americans **Native Americans** or **American Indians.** Study the timeline of early events in America:

First Americans cross land bridge	Dog domes- ticated	Farmers grow corn	Olmec Civiliza- tion (Mexico)		First city in America
23,000 B.C.	9000 B.C.	5000 B.C.	1000 B.C.	0	300 A.D.

7 Practice

A. Write the correct names on the map.

WORD BOX

Alaska	North America
Asia	Pacific Ocean
Bering Strait	South America
Central America	

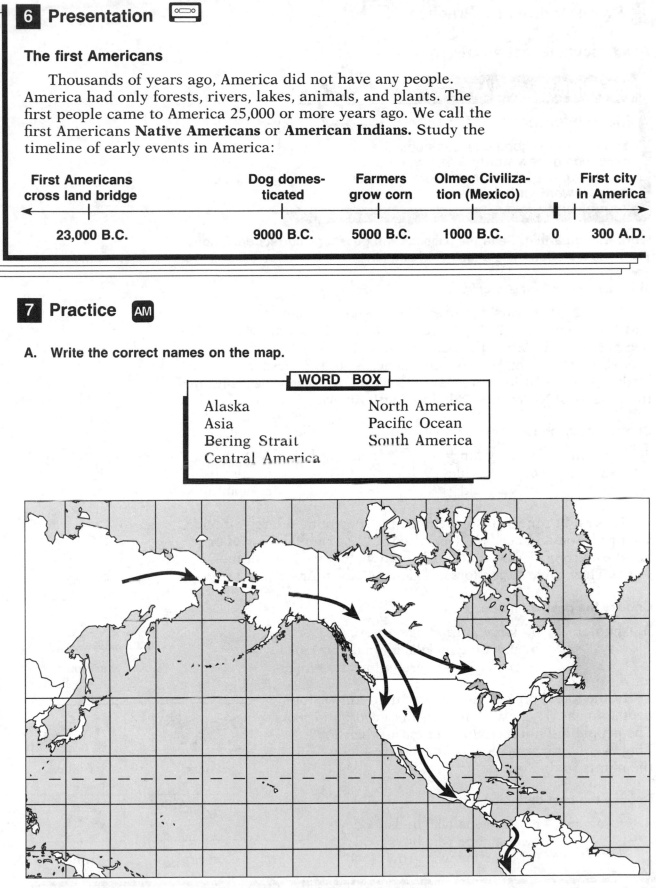

B. Guess: What continent did the first Americans come from?_____

8 Presentation and Practice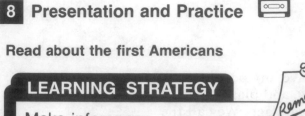

Read about the first Americans

> ### LEARNING STRATEGY
>
> **Make inferences**
>
> You can make good guesses about the meanings of new words. When you find a new word, read the words before and after the new word for help.

Work with a partner. Read the passage and guess the correct definitions. Then use a dictionary to check your answers.

Who were the first Americans?

About 25,000 years ago there was a land bridge between Asia and North America. Today there is no land bridge, only water. This body of water is called the Bering Strait. The first Americans probably went from Asia to America across this ancient land bridge. They went first to what is today Alaska. Then they migrated to all parts of North, Central, and South America.

Choose the best definition.

1. ancient
   a. very long
   b. very wide
   c. very old

2. migrated
   a. traveled
   b. discovered
   c. wanted

These first Americans were hunters. They hunted large animals, such as bison and caribou. One bison was enough food for many families. From Alaska, these early hunters followed the animals south. They came to the forest regions of North America.

bison

caribou

Choose the best definition.

3. hunter
   a. large animal like a bison
   b. person who kills animals for food
   c. person who lives in forest regions

In the forest regions, there were more things for people to eat. There were nuts, fruits, seeds, and roots. The people did not have to hunt for all their food. They were foragers. They looked for good food from the plants in the forests.

nuts **fruits**

Choose the best definition.

4. forager
   a. someone who finds food
   b. someone who buys food
   c. someone who grows food

seeds **roots**

Some Native Americans learned how to grow food plants. The first American farmers lived in the area that is today Mexico. They learned how to grow corn and other crops. Farming was important. People could live in one place, and they had more food.

Choose the best definition.

5. crops   **a.** a kind of corn
              b. plants and animals
              c. food that farmers grow

So Native Americans were hunters first. Then they were hunters and foragers. Finally, some Native Americans became farmers. They discovered some of the foods we eat today, such as corn, tomatoes, and potatoes.

Choose the best definition.

6. discover   **a.** eat something new
               b. find something new
               c. cook something new

The first Americans were part of prehistory. We know about them because of their artifacts, such as pottery and tools. We are still discovering new information about these early inhabitants of our continent.

9 Practice

LEARNING STRATEGY

Remember

Classify

Classifying helps you learn and remember information.

Classify information about the first Americans. Write the words in the correct column. Some words go in more than one column!

WORD BOX

Alaska	corn	land bridge	potatoes
~~Asia~~	crops	Mexico	roots
bison	forests	nuts	seeds
caribou	fruits	plants	tomatoes

HUNTERS	FORAGERS	FARMERS
Asia		

10 Presentation and Practice

Listen to information about the first people in North America. Circle the things the first Americans *had*. Cross out the things they did *not* have.

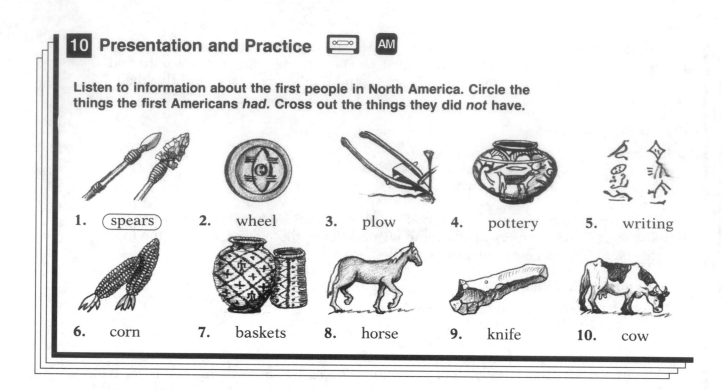

1. (spears)   2. wheel   3. plow   4. pottery   5. writing

6. corn   7. baskets   8. horse   9. knife   10. cow

11 Presentation

Read about early civilizations

┌─────────────── WORD BOX ───────────────┐

ancient: Very old, usually more than 1,000 years old.

artist: A person who produces works of art, such as paintings, sculpture, music, or literature.

civilization: An advanced human society with government, laws, values, education, and art.

domesticate: To make an animal live with and help humans.

engineer: A person who knows how to build things such as bridges, temples, and other buildings.

government: The political organization of a country or society.

impressive: Something that is wonderful and magnificent.

religion: A system of beliefs and values. Some of today's important religions are: Buddhism, Christianity, Islam, Judaism.

temple: A building for religious ceremonies.

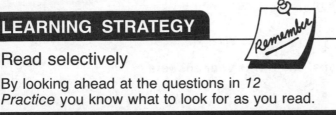

LEARNING STRATEGY

Read selectively

By looking ahead at the questions in *12 Practice* you know what to look for as you read.

Early Civilizations in the Middle East and Egypt

What is **civilization?** What are **civilized** people? A civilization is a group of people who have learned to live together in one place, to build cities, and to invent both beautiful and useful things. Civilized people have a system of government and a religion or philosophy.

Prehistoric people lived in many parts of the world a long time ago. They lived in Africa, in Asia, in Europe, and in the Middle East. You have read about how some of these prehistoric people traveled from Asia to North America and became the first Americans.

How did prehistoric people become part of history? When did people learn to write? When did civilization start? Look at the map. It shows part of the Middle East and Egypt. This is where the first cities and early civilizations started.

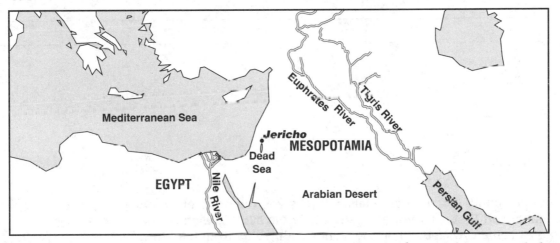

People settled near the rivers you see on the map. They had good farms, and they domesticated animals such as cows, horses, and sheep. People learned to live together, and they built the first cities. These cities had a government, laws, and religion.

Early civilizations in the Middle East and Egypt invented many important things. For example, the first writing started here. Other inventions that we still use today are the wheel, the plow, and the 365-day calendar. These early people also knew mathematics, and they were good engineers. They built very large and impressive buildings, such as temples and pyramids. We can still see some of these buildings today.

Ancient civilizations of the Middle East and Egypt had laws and schools. They also had artists who made many beautiful things such as paintings, sculptures, and jewelry. They wrote poetry and stories.

These early civilizations in the Middle East and Egypt were important in history. They invented many things that help people live better lives today. We know about these civilizations, because we can still see some of their buildings and we can study their artifacts. Even better, we can read about their lives and ideas, because they knew how to write.

12 Practice

Work with a partner. Discuss the questions. Then write your answers in complete sentences.

1. On what continents did prehistoric people live? _____

2. Where did the first civilized people live? _____

3. Why do you think early civilizations started near rivers? _____
   _____

4. Why do you think it was important to domesticate animals? _____
   _____

5. In your opinion, what were the three most useful things invented by early civilizations in the Middle East and Egypt? Why?

   _____

   _____

   _____

   _____

   _____

13 Practice

A sequence chain is a type of timeline. It tells you the order of events—
what happened first, second, next, etc. Study the sequence chain for
People Become Civilized. Fill in the blanks with words from the Word Box.

> **LEARNING STRATEGY**   *Remember*
>
> ### Use what you know
> Use the information that you have learned in
> this unit about history, ancient civilizations,
> and early Americans.

```
┌──────────────── WORD BOX ────────────────┐
│                                           │
│   animals      first      hunters   live  │
│   beautiful    food       invented  place │
│   domesticated government laws      work  │
│   farmers      grow       learned         │
│                                           │
└───────────────────────────────────────────┘
```

People become civilized

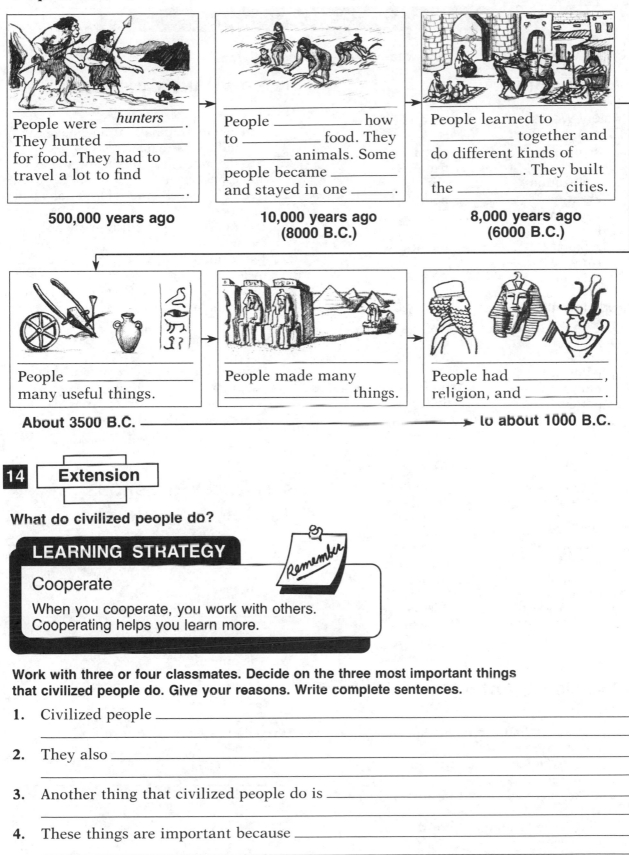

People were _____hunters_____.
They hunted _____
for food. They had to
travel a lot to find
_____.

500,000 years ago

People _____ how
to _____ food. They
_____ animals. Some
people became _____
and stayed in one _____.

**10,000 years ago
(8000 B.C.)**

People learned to
_____ together and
do different kinds of
_____. They built
the _____ cities.

**8,000 years ago
(6000 B.C.)**

People _____
many useful things.

About 3500 B.C.

People made many
_____ things.

People had _____,
religion, and _____.

to about 1000 B.C.

---

14 **Extension**

What do civilized people do?

LEARNING STRATEGY

Remember

Cooperate

When you cooperate, you work with others.
Cooperating helps you learn more.

**Work with three or four classmates. Decide on the three most important things
that civilized people do. Give your reasons. Write complete sentences.**

1. Civilized people _____
   _____

2. They also _____
   _____

3. Another thing that civilized people do is _____
   _____

4. These things are important because _____
   _____
   _____

UNIT 9: Learning Log

Check what you know. *Review* what you need to learn.

VOCABULARY

History Words
— A.D.
— artifact
— B.C.
— civilization
— event
— government
— law
— religion
— ruins
— timeline

Early Inventions/Art
— basket
— jewelry
— knife
— painting
— plow
— pottery
— pyramid
— sculpture
— spear
— temple
— wheel
— writing

Occupations
— archeologist
— artist
— engineer
— farmer
— forager
— hunter

Plants and Foods
— corn
— crops
— fruit
— nut
— potato
— root
— seed
— tomato

Animals
— bison
— caribou
— cow
— dog
— horse

Useful Past Tense Verbs
— built
— came
— discovered
— domesticated
— grew
— happened
— invented
— learned
— made
— migrated
— traveled
— wrote

Adjectives
— ancient
— beautiful
— impressive

LEARNING STRATEGIES

I can:
— Use what I know to understand new information.
— Understand and make a timeline.
— Read selectively.
— Make inferences about meanings of new words.
— Classify information about the first Americans.
— Cooperate with classmates.

CONTENT AND LANGUAGE

I can:
— Talk about and make a timeline of my life and a classmate's life.
— Use the past tense to talk and write about past events.
— Read and understand information about history.
— Use the simple present to write about facts.
— Use a timeline to solve problems about historical events.
— Read, listen, and understand information about the first Americans.
— Read and answer questions about early civilizations in the Middle East and Egypt.
— Complete a sequence chain about how people became civilized.
— Write about the characteristics of civilized people.

SELF-CHECK QUESTIONS

What is interesting in Unit 9?

_____

_____

What is easy?

_____

_____

What is difficult?

_____

_____

How can you learn what is difficult?

_____

_____

Folktales of the World

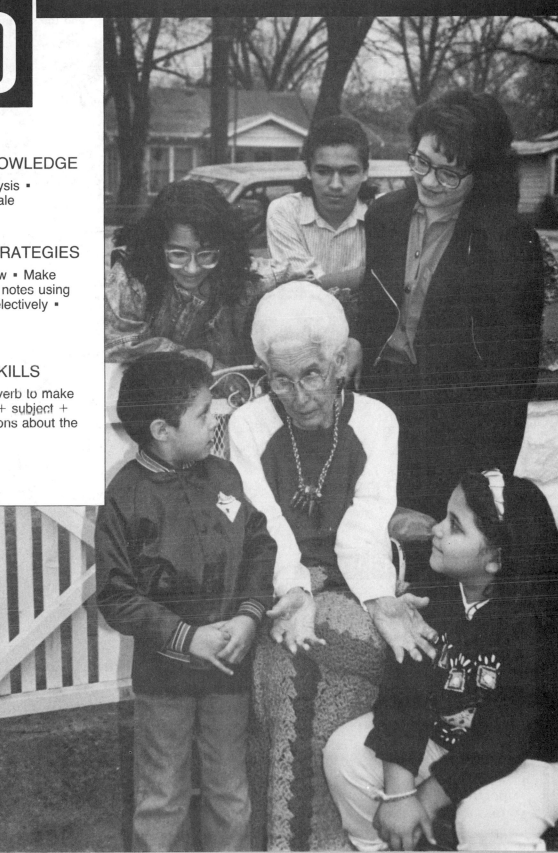

CONTENT KNOWLEDGE

Using literary analysis ▪
Interpreting a folktale

LEARNING STRATEGIES

Use what you know ▪ Make
inferences ▪ Take notes using
a T-list ▪ Listen selectively ▪
Make predictions

LANGUAGE SKILLS

Be + going to + verb to make
predictions ▪ *Did + subject +
verb* to ask questions about the
past

1 Preparation

What do you already know about stories?

Oh, we're going to read more stories in this unit. I bet we're going to talk about characters and the setting and . . .

Match the words in the Word Box with their definitions.

> **WORD BOX**
>
> event   plot   ~~character~~
> setting   problem   fable

1. ___*character*___ An important person in the story
2. _____ Where the story takes place
3. _____ What needs to be solved in a story
4. _____ A story with a moral
5. _____ Something that happens in the story
6. _____ All the things that happen in a story

2 Presentation

What is a folktale?

Every country has its stories. Fathers and mothers tell these stories to their children and to each other. There is a special kind of story called a **folktale.** Folktales are part of each country's history, culture, and traditions. Folktales usually tell us about the people in a country—what they believe, what they do with their lives, what is important to them. Folktales can be about dreams, adventures, the old teaching the young, or about strange or frightening events.

In the past, most folktales were not written down. They were told orally, one person telling another. People told these stories for many reasons, sometimes to explain nature and sometimes to stop people from breaking nature's laws. People also told folktales to make the listener want to be kind, unselfish, or brave. And, of course, people told folktales for fun!

Recently, **anthropologists,** or scientists who study the growth and culture of man, began to visit other countries, talk to the people, and write down their folktales. And soon the anthropologists found out an interesting thing. Tales from different countries often have similar plots! This means that all over the world, different people have similar thoughts, questions, problems, and dreams.

3 Practice AM

LEARNING STRATEGY

Remember

Take notes

Taking notes on a T-list is a good way to organize new information. When you take notes, write only the most important words.

A. Use the T-list below to take notes on *2 Presentation*.

Title : Folktales

What folktales are	A. Stories told by parents to
	B. Part of each country's _____
	C. Tell us about people in country : what they believe, _____
	_____
why people tell folktales	A. _____
	B. _____
	C. _____
	D. _____
Facts about folktales	A. In past, told _____ , not in writing.
	B. Anthropologists visited _____
	C. Anthropologists found _____
	D. People have _____

B. Now check your work with a classmate.

4 Presentation

Read a folktale from Mexico

The Rider and the Brambles

This forest, people said, was haunted with ghosts and scary things.

A man was riding his horse, going home one evening. To get home, he had to ride through a forest.

When the rider went into the forest, he suddenly felt hands on his waist! The hands were so strong, he couldn't get away! He was so scared, he couldn't breathe. He spent the night there, caught in the huge hands!

Finally, day came. In the light, he saw no hands. He was caught in some brambles.

5 Practice

Now answer these questions about the story.

1. What is the title of the folktale? _The Rider and the Brambles_____

2. Who is the main character? _____

3. Where is the character going? _____

4. What is the setting? _____

5. What do people in the story say about the setting? _____

6. What does *haunted* mean? _____

7. The rider can't get through the forest. What does he think is happening? _____
   _____

8. What does the rider do? _____

9. Day comes. What does the rider find out? _____
   _____

10. Which sentence below best tells the moral of the story?
    a. Get home before dark.
    b. Don't go into a haunted forest.
    c. Your imagination can be very strong.
    d. You see things clearly during the day.

11. What type of folktale is this?
    a. A folktale about a dream.
    b. A folktale about a strange and frightening event.
    c. A folktale about not breaking the laws of nature.
    d. A folktale about the old teaching the young.

6 Presentation 📼 AM

Listen to a folktale

You are going to listen to a folktale two times. The first time, just listen. The second time, fill in the missing words in the story below.

LEARNING STRATEGY

Remember

Listen selectively

Don't forget to read the story *before* you listen. What words are missing? The second time you listen, listen carefully for these words.

This folktale is about a man named Nasrudin. Nasrudin was a very

_____*funny*_____ man, with an unusual sense of humor. He was also

very _____ .

One day, three small boys made a _____ . They wanted to

_____ , or take, Nasrudin's _____ and run away.

So they called to him and said, "Look at that _____ . No one can

_____ , it's too tall."

Nasrudin smiled. "Each of you can _____ ," he said. "Anyone

can, really. I'll show you."

Before Nasrudin began to climb the tree, he took off his _____ .

But he didn't leave them on the ground. He put them _____ . And

then he started to climb.

The boys exclaimed, "Mulla, you don't need _____ in a

_____ ! Leave them here!"

But Nasrudin would not. He knew the boys wanted _____ . He

said, "You have to be _____ for everything. Maybe I'll find a

_____ up here, and I'll need those _____ !"

Now answer these questions about the story of Nasrudin. Choose the correct letter.

1. What type of person is Nasrudin?
   a. Smart
   b. Funny
   c. Prepared
   d. All of the above

2. The boys had a plan. What was it?
   a. They wanted to climb the tree.
   b. They wanted to steal Nasrudin's shoes.
   c. They wanted to see if Nasrudin could climb the tree.
   d. They wanted to take the road and see where it went.

3. Why did the boys want Nasrudin to climb the tree?
   a. They wanted to know if there was a road in the tree.
   b. They wanted him to take off his shoes.
   c. They didn't think anyone could climb the tree.
   d. They wanted to climb the tree themselves.

4. Why did Nasrudin put his shoes in his pocket?
   a. He needed the shoes for walking.
   b. He didn't want to wear the shoes in the tree.
   c. He didn't want the boys to steal the shoes.
   d. He only had one pair of shoes.

5. Nasrudin guessed the boys' plan. Why didn't he tell them so?
   a. He wanted to trick them.
   b. He wasn't a brave man.
   c. He wanted to climb the tree.
   d. He thought their plan was clever.

6. What's a good title for this story?
   a. Be funny
   b. Climbing trees
   c. Be prepared
   d. The road in the tree

8 Presentation

Read another Nasrudin story

Nasrudin stories are told in many parts of the world—Turkey, Greece, Sicily, and the Soviet Union, for example. One group of religious people called the Sufis use Nasrudin stories as mental exercises. They tell the stories again and again, and think about their favorite ones. They believe that they can find great wisdom and truth in the stories.

There are many Nasrudin stories. In fact, people say that it is impossible to tell just one Nasrudin story. So here is another!

Why?

It was a hot summer day, and Nasrudin was lying under a mulberry tree. There were some very large watermelons nearby.

Nasrudin looked at the watermelons, and he thought, "That's strange. Here is this giant, beautiful mulberry tree. Yet it produces such tiny fruit. And there's a plant that doesn't grow tall, it just moves along the ground. So silly . . . yet it produces such big, delicious melons. I wonder why?"

As Nasrudin was thinking about this strange fact of nature, a mulberry fell on his head. Nasrudin smiled. "Oh, I see," he said. "That's the reason! It's so obvious, I should have thought of it at once!"

9 Practice

A. Complete these sentences. Some words are suggested in the Word Box.

┌── WORD BOX ──┐

small	hot	cloudy	rainy	summer	watermelon
mulberry	tall	delicious	big	~~Nasrudin~~	beautiful

1. The main character is ___Nasrudin_____ .

2. The setting is _____ .

3. Mulberry trees are _____ .

4. The fruit of the mulberry tree is a _____ .

5. Watermelons are _____ .

6. Nasrudin compares mulberry trees to the _____ plants.

B. Now answer these questions about the story.

1. When Nasrudin asks "why," he is thinking nature is wrong. Which picture shows his idea of how nature should be? _____ .

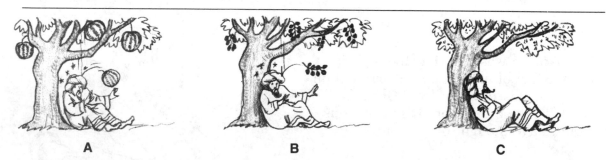

   A   B   C

2. What is one event in the story? _____

   _____

3. A mulberry falls on Nasrudin's head. He sees that nature is right, after all. But imagine that Nasrudin's first idea was the way of nature. What would happen?

   _____

   A   B   C

4. What type of folktale is this?
   a. A folktale about a dream.
   b. A folktale about a strange and frightening event.
   c. A folktale about not breaking the laws of nature.
   d. A folktale to explain the laws of nature.

10 Presentation 📼

This folktale is from Africa. Read the beginning of the story.

The Dog Who Would Be King

The people liked Mr. Dog because he was so friendly. They wanted to make Mr. Dog the king of their land. So they looked for all of the things that a king should have. They found a crown, rings, and the skin of the mukaka, which is a small animal. When all was ready, they said, "The day has come. We will make Mr. Dog king."

Every important person came. They brought players of the drum and marimba. They put down beautiful mats to sit on. They had delicious food to eat, lots of chicken and vegetables and fruit. Then Mr. Dog came in. Everyone was standing at attention. They had a beautiful chair for Mr. Dog. "Let the lord sit," they said. Mr. Dog sat down.

11 Practice AM

Put these pictures in order, so they tell the story.

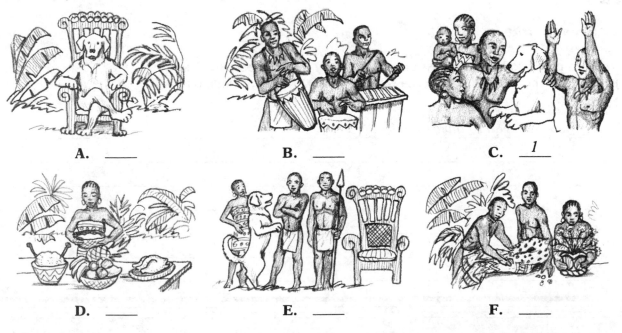

A. ____   B. ____   C. *1*

D. ____   E. ____   F. ____

12 Practice

**Work with a partner. Write several sentences about what is going to
happen next. Remember to use what you know about dogs!**

LANGUAGE SKILL

To make a prediction, use **be (not)** + **going to** + *verb*.

Mr. Dog **is going to bite** an important person.
The people **are not going to like** Mr. Dog.

_____

_____

_____

_____

_____

13 Presentation and Practice

Listen and write

**You are going to hear the next part of the story three times. The first time,
just listen. The second time, write what you hear. The third time, check
your work.**

The people began to divide the food.

_____

_____

_____

_____

_____

_____

14 Practice

Answer the questions below about the African folktale.

```
┌─────────── LANGUAGE  SKILL ───────────┐
│                                        │
│  Use did + subject + verb to ask       │
│  questions about the past.             │
│                                        │
│    Why did the people want Mr. Dog to  │
│    be their King?                      │
│                                        │
│  Use subject + past tense verb to      │
│  answer questions about the past.      │
│                                        │
│    The people wanted Mr. Dog to be     │
│    their king, because he was so       │
│    friendly.                           │
│                                        │
└────────────────────────────────────────┘
```

1. Why did the people want Mr. Dog to be their king?

   _____

2. What things did they think a king should have? _____

   _____

3. What did the people do to get ready for the big day? _____

   _____

4. Who came? _____

5. Where did Mr. Dog sit? _____

6. Which picture shows what Mr. Dog did? _____

A   B   C

7. The people decided not to make Mr. Dog their king. Why?

   _____

8. What *should* Mr. Dog have done, if he wanted to be king?

   _____

9. What type of folktale is this?
   a. A folktale about a strange and frightening event.
   b. A folktale to make the listener a better person.
   c. A folktale to explain the laws of nature.
   d. A folktale about not breaking the laws of nature.

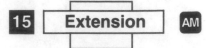

Be a storyteller

A. Folktales, as you know, are stories people *tell* to one another. Be a storyteller and tell a group of your classmates a folktale. You can tell a folktale from this Unit, or you can tell a folktale from your country. You decide! (If you decide to tell a folktale from this Unit, *don't* look back in the book. Use your memory.)

Think about the folktale first. What is the title? Who are the characters? What is the setting? What happens in the story? Make notes to yourself below. List important vocabulary you need. Don't write out the whole story—just make notes!

_____

_____

_____

_____

_____

_____

B. Now meet with two classmates. Each person should tell his or her story. Be a good storyteller—make the story exciting and interesting! When your classmates have told their stories, take notes below on their stories.

	CLASSMATE 1'S STORY	CLASSMATE 2'S STORY
Title:	_____	_____
Where the story is from:	_____	_____
Characters:	_____	_____
	_____	_____
Setting:	_____	_____
Some events:	_____	_____
	_____	_____
	_____	_____
	_____	_____
The ending:	_____	_____
The point:	_____	_____
What type of folktale is this?	_____	_____

UNIT 10: Learning Log

Check what you know. *Review* what you need to learn.

VOCABULARY

Story Words
— character
— event
— fable
— folktale
— moral
— plot
— problem
— setting
— storyteller
— title

Special People
— anthropologists
— Nasrudin
— Sufis

Animals
— chicken
— dog
— horse

Nouns
— adventures
— brambles
— crown
— dreams
— forest
— ghosts
— imagination
— mulberry
— nature
— pocket
— truth
— watermelon
— wisdom

Useful Past Tense Verbs
— began
— fell
— felt
— found out
— made
— spent
— told
— took off

Adjectives
— brave
— frightening
— haunted
— kind
— scared
— smart
— unselfish

Verbs
— breathe
— climb
— divide
— produce
— steal

LEARNING STRATEGIES

I can:
— Use what I know to understand new information.
— Make inferences about a story.
— Take notes using a T-list.
— Listen selectively.
— Make predictions about what is going to happen next.

CONTENT AND LANGUAGE

I can:
— Read and understand information about folktales.
— Read and answer questions about folktales.
— Put story events in order.
— Use **be** + **going to** + *verb* to make predictions.
— Take dictation.
— Use **did** + *subject* + *verb* to ask questions.
— Use *subject* + *past tense* to answer questions.
— Be a storyteller.

SELF-CHECK QUESTIONS

What is interesting in Unit 10?

_____
_____

What is easy?

_____
_____

What is difficult?

_____
_____

How can you learn what is difficult?

_____
_____

Learning Strategies: Book 2

LEARNING STRATEGY	PRESENTED	REENTERED
Use what you know	Unit 1, p. 2	Unit 2, pp. 14, 21 Unit 3, p. 28 Unit 4, p. 42 Unit 5, p. 55 Unit 6, p. 72 Unit 7, p. 83 Unit 8, p. 96 Unit 9, pp. 108, 118 Unit 10, p. 122
Make inferences	Unit 1, p. 7	Unit 6, pp. 74, 77 Unit 8, p. 96 Unit 9, p. 114 Unit 10, p. 122
Read selectively	Unit 1, p. 9	Unit 5, p. 59 Unit 8, pp. 101, 102, 104 Unit 9, pp. 110, 117
Cooperate	Unit 1, p. 10	Unit 3, p. 38 Unit 5, p. 57 Unit 7, p. 92 Unit 8, p. 101 Unit 9, p. 119
Classify	Unit 2, p. 17	Unit 2, p. 20 Unit 3, pp. 33, 36 Unit 9, p. 115
Listen selectively	Unit 2, p. 18	Unit 3, p. 34 Unit 4, p. 43 Unit 5, p. 68 Unit 6, p. 79 Unit 7, p. 88 Unit 8, p. 98 Unit 10, p. 125

Take notes:
   Idea Maps
 	
   Story Maps
   T-list
 	
   Diagram
   General
	
	Unit 3, p. 30
	
	Unit 4, p. 49
	Unit 6, p. 79
	
	Unit 7, p. 87
		
		Unit 3, pp. 31, 32
		Unit 6, p. 76
		Unit 7, p. 84
		Unit 4, pp. 50, 51, 52
		Unit 8, p. 105
		Unit 10, p. 123
		
		Unit 8, p. 98

Make predictions	Unit 4, p. 46	Unit 10, p. 130
Write a summary	Unit 4, p. 50	Unit 4, p. 51
Make a picture or table	Unit 5, p. 56	
Math word problem strategies	Unit 5, p. 61	Unit 5, p. 62
Make a timeline	Unit 9, p. 109	Unit 9, p. 112

Language Skills and Vocabulary Sets
Book 2

LANGUAGE SKILLS AND VOCABULARY SETS	UNIT									
	1	2	3	4	5	6	7	8	9	10
Adjectives	x		x	x						
Adjective + noun						x				
Be + going to + verb										x
Because/too			x							
Can + verb								x		
Did + subject + verb										x
Direction words		x								
Five senses	x									
Have/has to + verb								x		
History										
Civilization									x	
Inventions									x	
Time									x	
Timelines									x	
How many/how much					x					
Imperatives	x									
Literary analysis				x						x
Living things:										
Animals							x			
Cells							x			
Characteristics							x			
Plants							x			
Mapping/Geography:										
Climate						x				
Continents		x								
Countries		x								
Oceans		x								
Rivers/lakes		x								
Map scales		x								
Vegetation						x				
World regions						x				

LANGUAGE SKILLS AND VOCABULARY SETS	UNIT									
	1	2	3	4	5	6	7	8	9	10
Math:										
Area					x					
Averages					x					
Division					x					
Geometric shapes					x					
Multiplication					x					
Word problems					x					
Nutrition:										
Calories			x							
Food groups			x							
Foods			x							
Nutrients			x							
Ordinal numbers			x							
Past tense:										
Irregular verbs	x			x			x			
Past continuous				x						
Regular verbs	x			x			x			
Statements & Qs	x		x		x				x	
Present continuous	x									
Scientific Method	x									
Should + verb								x		
Simple present	x	x	x	x	x	x	x		x	
U.S. Society:										
Government								x		
Laws								x		
Rights & responsibilities								x		
Where's?		x								
Why/because								x		

VOCABULARY

The following list contains words used in *Building Bridges, Book 2*, and the page numbers where the words are actively used.